THE WELFARE SYSTEM

*Help or
Hindrance
to the Poor?*

Marianne LeVert

*Issue and Debate
The Millbrook Press
Brookfield, Connecticut*

Photographs courtesy of AP/Wide World Photos: pp. 9, 25, 29, 42, 58, 68; Impact Visuals: pp. 12 (Edward Peters), 39 (Robert Fox), 49 (Harvey Finkle), 54 (Harvey Finkle), 65 (Evan Johnson), 73 (Linda Rosier), 81 (Catherine Smith), 93 (Vic Hinterland), 98 (J. Kirk Condyles); Bettmann: pp. 21, 77, 85.

Library of Congress Cataloging-in-Publication Data
LeVert, Marianne.
The welfare system : help or hindrance to the poor? /
Marianne LeVert.
p.   cm.—(Issue and debate)
Includes bibliographical references and index.
Summary: An examination of our welfare system: how it has evolved, its complex character at present, and the thorny issue of what the government should do now to better help the poor.
ISBN 1-56294-455-X
1. Public welfare—United States—Juvenile literature.   2. Public welfare administration—United States—Juvenile literature.
3. United States—Social policy—Juvenile literature.   I. Series.
HV91.L388   1995   361.6'0973—dc20   94-21815   CIP   AC

Published by The Millbrook Press, Inc.
2 Old New Milford Road, Brookfield, Connecticut 06804

Contents

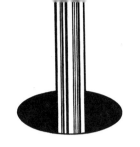

The Welfare System

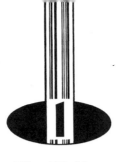

The Welfare
Dilemma

On April 29, 1992, a Los Angeles jury acquitted four white police officers accused of assaulting black motorist Rodney King during his arrest for speeding. This verdict was the extremely controversial culmination of a case that had drawn the nation into a heated debate about police brutality, justice, and racial discrimination. Many people believed that our justice system had failed. Some took their anger to the streets.

In the south-central section of Los Angeles, an area of the city where many blacks and Hispanics live in desperate poverty and isolation, stores were looted, buildings were burned, motorists were dragged from their cars, and bystanders were beaten. Protests spread across the county, but Los Angeles, the site of the assault and the subsequent trial, experienced the most devastating damage and loss: More than 13,000 people were arrested, at least 2,100 were injured, and 58 were killed. Property damage was estimated at about $1 billion. Although not the first, it was the worst domestic disturbance of the century.

Having viewed a graphic and disturbing videotape of the arrest and beating of King on national television, most Americans, regardless of their race, disagreed with the jury's decision.[1] Most, however, were equally stunned by the violence and destruction that swept through the streets of our cities. What, they asked, were the roots of such discontent? To answer this question, the nation focused its attention on the serious racial, social, and economic problems in our country: crime, violence, the breakup of the family, racial discrimination, poverty, urban decay, and welfare dependency.

In their search for the underlying causes of this kind of social unrest, concerned Americans took a close look at the terrible poverty and despair that were affecting millions of families, especially in our inner cities. They found that in Los Angeles, as in every major city in the country, unemployment, school failure, child poverty, teen pregnancy, and out-of-wedlock birthrates were at their highest levels in thirty years. A record number of Americans throughout the United States were dependent on government assistance—welfare—to support themselves and their families.

Many analysts believed that these distressing social and economic conditions not only contributed directly to the kind of social unrest witnessed in Los Angeles, but also signified a terrible failure of our government's social policies and programs. Although policy experts, child advocates, lawmakers, and the public all recommended changes, there was little consensus about what path the government should take. Some believed that the government had done too little to help the poor. They recommended increasing supportive, educational, and economic aid so that more families could avoid or

On December 28, 1993, a homeless man drags his belongings across Lafayette Park in front of the United States Treasury Department.

escape poverty. Others argued that the government already gave too much to the poor. They wanted to see our welfare system restrict benefits and demand more personal effort and responsibility from its recipients.

What Is Welfare? According to polls, most Americans considered our welfare system "a failure and a disgrace."[2] This opinion, however, reflected more a lack of faith in our current system than an unwillingness to help others: When Americans were asked if they thought that our government spent too much money on the poor, only 17 percent said yes; 32 percent, however, said they thought that the government spent too much money on welfare.[3]

Our social welfare system is composed of hundreds of state and federal programs designed to meet the needs of American citizens. Some, including Social Security, Medicare, Unemployment Insurance, and Workers' Compensation, are called social insurance programs because they aim to insure citizens against the loss of their income as a result of age, unemployment, or injury. Because recipients of these programs have contributed toward their benefits during their working years, social insurance programs are generally considered rewards for work, or entitlements (government programs that provide benefits to those who are entitled to them).

Most people use the word "welfare" to mean income support or public assistance programs designed to help people who are already poor. These are income-tested or means-tested programs and include Aid to Families with Dependent Children, Food Stamps, Medicaid, and Supplemental Security Insurance. Both social insurance and public assistance programs provide cash—usually monthly grants—and noncash or "in-kind" benefits, including medical insurance, food supplements, and other goods and services.

Although some states offer small General Assistance payments to single individuals, few able-bodied adults without children are eligible for public assistance. Aid to Families with Dependent Children (AFDC) is the largest of our means-tested programs and is commonly the focus of heated debate about welfare. AFDC provides monthly cash grants to poor single-parent households, about 88 percent of whom are headed by women without incomes adequate to support their families. Because their incomes are so low, AFDC recipients automatically qualify for Food Stamps and Medicaid, as well as other services. Although some recipients are divorced or separated, an alarming 54 percent have never been married. AFDC-UP (Unemployed Parent), which was created to encourage family stability by providing benefits to two-parent families when the primary earner is unemployed, accounts for only a small number of recipients.

Of the more than 32 million Americans considered officially poor by the U.S. government in 1993, about 14 million, mostly children, depended on AFDC for support. Approximately 2,000 children a day join the welfare rolls. Most of these children will spend at least two years supported by the government, and at least 25 percent of them will remain on welfare for more than five years. Few will ever live with their father or receive financial support from him. Senator Daniel Patrick Moynihan, a leading authority on welfare policy, estimates that, if current trends continue, one out of three children born after 1980 will, at some point in life, be on public assistance.[4]

Although benefits vary from state to state, the average monthly AFDC grant is less than $400 a month. Living well below what the government considers the poverty level, families on welfare often relate feelings of hopelessness, shame, and despair. "It strips you of

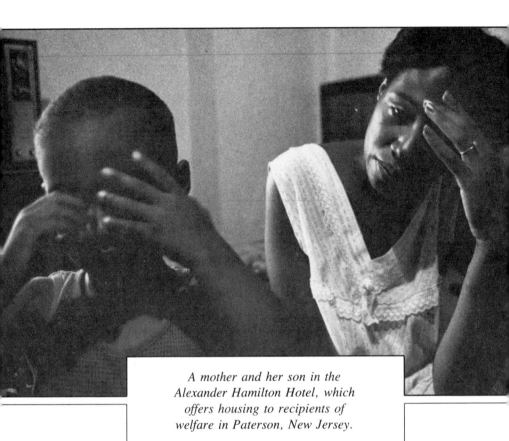

A mother and her son in the
Alexander Hamilton Hotel, which
offers housing to recipients of
welfare in Paterson, New Jersey.

your dignity," one welfare mother of two children says about the welfare system. "It feels like I'm in a sea drowning and there's no way out."[5] By far, the majority of recipients would rather work than collect welfare. The road from welfare to self-support, however, is often filled with difficulties: finding a job that pays a decent wage, obtaining adequate child support from fathers, affording quality day care for children, and obtaining essential medical insurance. For many, especially those with little education and few skills, employment does not necessarily mean greater financial security.

The Conservative View. Many conservative analysts, who generally believe that the federal government should play a limited role in social and economic matters, contend that the government should not support citizens who are physically and mentally capable of working. Since the majority of single mothers, including those with young children, are currently working outside the home, they argue that society has no inherent obligation to support single mothers who do not work. AFDC, many believe, encourages the formation of single-parent families as well as long-term welfare use, or dependency. Most people on this side of the debate believe that our government should restrict the period of time a person can collect benefits, impose work requirements, and limit the number of children the government will support in a family. Some recommend eliminating AFDC altogether.

Lawrence Mead, associate professor of politics at New York University and author of *The New Politics of Poverty: The Nonworking Poor in America,* says that the problems of today's poor are beyond the reach of government programs. This, he claims, is because chronic poverty is principally the result of self-defeating behaviors among the poor themselves, rather than the result of economic, racial, or social factors. According to Mead, these behaviors, including having children without the benefit of marriage or financial means, dropping out of school, and accepting welfare for long periods of time rather than seeking employment, should not be rewarded with government subsidies.

After the Los Angeles riots, and throughout the 1992 presidential campaign, many analysts linked the growth of poverty to the growth of single-parent households in our society, especially those in which the mother was never married. Although experts from both sides of the welfare debate acknowledge that poverty is closely linked to family composition—single-parent families experience poverty at six times the rate of intact families—conservative thinkers commonly blame the decline of traditional family structure on a decline in moral standards rather than on economic or cultural influences. Former Vice President Dan Quayle, in fact, touched off a fierce national debate about poverty and family structure when he criticized widespread acceptance of unwed motherhood and linked the unrest in Los Angeles to a "poverty of values" in our culture.[6]

William J. Bennett, former secretary of education under President Ronald Reagan and current fellow at the Hudson Institute and the Heritage Foundation, two conservative think tanks, also argued that moral decay was at the heart of our social and economic problems.

What happened in the streets of Los Angeles is, at bottom, not about economic poverty. For parts of the city, the road to disaster has been paved by a corrosive popular culture, educational failure, moral and spiritual depletion and the breakdown of our most critical institution—the family. . . . This moral decay is in part the result of a disastrous 25-year experiment—boys growing up in a nihilistic culture without the presence of their fathers, few positive male role models, terrible schools and feckless churches—in other words, few civilizing influences. We should not be shocked when these boys do not grow up to be good and decent men.[7]

The experiment he cites was the federal government's effort to address the needs of the poor by creating new welfare programs and expanding the already existing welfare and antipoverty programs during the 1960s and 1970s. Some conservative thinkers contend that these measures have not only failed to improve the quality of life for disadvantaged Americans, but have instead actually helped to create a permanently poor group of citizens. This, they charge, is because welfare programs discourage hard work, individual initiative, and family planning. Many believe that our welfare system should include strict work requirements, time limits, and rewards for marriage.

The Liberal View. On the other side of the debate are liberal thinkers, who generally believe that government has a fundamental responsibility for the well-being of all its citizens, including the poor. Most of these analysts blame economic trends and racial barriers—not character flaws or personal behavior—for the rise of poverty and welfare dependency.

While agreeing that increases in the number of single-parent families are directly related to increases in poverty and welfare dependency, experts on this side of the argument contend that this relationship is tied not to the availability of welfare benefits but to poor economic prospects for spouses, low pay for women, insufficient child support for children, and inadequate government support for poor single parents. Many suggest helping single parents become self-sufficient by boosting services and income support, not by curtailing or eliminating this kind of help. Imposing further hardships on needy families, asserts Senator Moynihan, is tantamount to telling innocent children to "shape up or starve."[8]

Marian Wright Edelman, founder of the Children's Defense Fund, acknowledges that there has been a "breakdown in values in all of our society." At the same time, however, she is critical of those who espouse "rhetoric about family values, and then not being for good prenatal care, not being for universal health insurance, not being for full funding for Head Start. There's a heck of a lot of hypocrisy to mouth family values when you don't support the things families need to keep themselves together."[9] She worries that cutting back on aid will only punish the poor and further deprive their children. Instead of blaming the victims of poverty for their predicament, she would like to see the government help welfare recipients become self-sufficient by increasing supportive services such as education, medical insurance, day care subsidies, job training, and employment opportunities.

Michael B. Katz, author of *The Undeserving Poor,* agrees with this position, saying that "citizens should expect the resources essential for learning, work, and family life if they are to avoid low SAT scores, unemployment, adolescent pregnancy, and welfare dependency. These resources include adequate schools, affordable housing, reasonably priced day care, guaranteed health care, and decent jobs. In American cities, poor people can count on none of these."[10]

Examining the Issues. The subject of welfare often triggers heated emotional debate. Some Americans do not believe that able-bodied adults deserve public assistance and resent paying taxes to support those who do not work. This sentiment has become more common since the majority of women with children, both married and single, now work outside the home. Unfortunately, public resentment of welfare programs and their recipients sometimes stems from prejudice, misinformation, and the acceptance of stereotypes of welfare recipients.

In general, however, dissatisfaction with welfare programs does not stem from overt racism, selfishness, or indifference toward those who are less fortunate. On the contrary, our country has a long history of compassion and generosity. Community spirit, family ties, volunteerism, and charity work are integral to the American way of life.

At the same time, pride in hard work and individual effort and responsibility are deeply embedded in our national character. Welfare, then, presents a dilemma for Americans who want to help the needy but who also believe that the poor should make every effort to help themselves. How do we decide which poor Americans are doing the best they can to support themselves? Who, in other words, deserves our help?

In order to know if and how our current system has failed, we need to examine the goals of public welfare and how these goals have responded to our changing society. How effective are programs designed to help the poor? What obligation does the government have to the needy? And what do recipients owe society in return? What, if anything, can our government do to solve the problem of poverty in America? How much are we willing to do? These are questions that our society has been trying to answer for a long time.

The Evolution
of Welfare

Our modern welfare system is composed of a myriad of social insurance, public assistance, and antipoverty programs designed to benefit American citizens. This system, however, was not created until the 1930s. For almost three centuries of our history, local, state, and federal governments offered only meager help to those considered the most needy and the most deserving.

Colonial Poor Laws. The first Europeans to settle in America were Puritans, who viewed hard work and material success as religious virtues. Idleness was considered a vice; except for the weak or the old, all were expected to support themselves and their families. Although plentiful land and abundant resources promised a better life for the colonists, many of whom came here impoverished, not all newcomers prospered. Life in America was difficult, and hardship and poverty were widespread despite the settlers' hard work. In addition, many settlers were unable to provide for themselves:

the sick, the elderly, the disabled, and widows with children.

Faced with the task of deciding who deserved assistance and who was responsible for the poor, each of the thirteen colonies enacted various "poor laws." Based on similar laws in England, these colonial poor laws established relief policy for the next three centuries and laid the foundation for our modern welfare system. These laws required local communities to care for their needy residents. Although families were primarily responsible for the care and support of their dependents, each household was required to pay a tax to aid needy people who lacked family support.

Help was extended only to people whose need was due to conditions beyond their control—sickness, age, mental or physical illness, and widowhood. Helpless to change their circumstances and not expected by the larger society to work, these were the "worthy" poor. Able-bodied adults without means of support, on the other hand, were not only ineligible for aid but were also scorned and severely punished. Beggars could be whipped, imprisoned, branded, or even executed. "For those who indulge in idleness," said religious leader Cotton Mather, "the express command of God unto us is, that we should let them starve."[1]

The colonists enacted strict laws to keep poor people—or even those the community feared might become poor—from settling in their towns. These strangers were "warned out" or escorted to the town's borders. As the country's population swelled over the next century, new cities and towns developed and mobility increased, making it more difficult for towns to take responsibility for their residents. As a result, the county and, in the nineteenth century, individual states, assumed responsibility for assisting the needy.

Indoor and Outdoor Relief. From our earliest history, the notion of giving cash and goods to indigent individuals and families in their homes was controversial. Community leaders warned that "outdoor relief," as this practice was called, diminished a person's work effort and destroyed his or her moral character. In 1821, Josiah Quincy, the mayor of Boston, claimed: "Of all the modes of providing for the poor, the most wasteful, the most expensive, and the most injurious to their morals and destructive to their industrious habits is that of supply in their own families."[2]

By the early 1800s, the belief that cash assistance was detrimental to a poor person's character prompted communities to curtail or eliminate outdoor relief in favor of "indoor" relief, or institutional care—workhouses for the able-bodied and almshouses for the helpless poor. Institutions for the aged, the blind and handicapped, the mentally ill, and the orphans and children of the poor were common by the end of the century.

Reforms. Despite the dramatic changes that took place during the 1800s and early 1900s—the arrival of more than 21 million immigrants and the rapid growth of industries and cities—there remained no government or employer system of protection against destitution for American citizens. Low wages, periodic economic downturns, unsafe working conditions, sickness, and old age plunged countless families into poverty.

Scores of private charities, religious foundations, and fraternal organizations attempted to meet the needs of our cities' growing immigrant and working-class population. Many charity workers, called "paternal guardians" and "friendly visitors," provided spiritual guidance to correct what they considered the "moral deficiencies"

Newsboys lie huddled in a corner outside a church, taking a break from their lives on the streets. Photograph by Jacob Riis, about 1890.

of the poor. A growing number of social reformers, however, sought to improve health, housing, and working conditions for children and workers.

Although progress was slow, by the turn of the century several states had passed laws to provide cash assistance to various categories of needy citizens. In 1898, Ohio established a state pension for the blind, and in 1915, Alaska passed the country's first law for aid to the aged. By 1920, some forty-three states had enacted legislation that entitled workers who were injured on the job to compensation. Efforts to provide unemployment insurance, however, would not be successful until the next decade.

The Welfare of Children and Widows. The welfare of children was integral to the emerging reform movement in the early 1900s. Poor children toiled in factories, were at the mercy of a justice system designed for adults, and, especially if the mother was the sole provider, were commonly placed in institutions or foster homes. In 1909, appalled by these disturbing conditions, President Theodore Roosevelt convened a White House Conference on Dependent Children. This two-day conference, attended by more than two hundred child advocates, signaled for the first time a willingness on the part of the federal government to intervene on behalf of needy citizens.

Pointing to the devastating consequences of separating poor children from their mothers, the attendees urged the federal government to provide the means to keep families together. Such measures, they argued, would benefit all of society. As one social worker stated, "Home life is the highest and finest product of civilization. It is a great molding force of mind and of character. Children should not be deprived of it except for urgent and compelling reasons."[3]

Although the federal government did not create a national assistance program for single mothers, several states did begin providing cash assistance for widowed mothers. In 1911, Illinois passed the country's first mothers' aid law, the Funds to Parents Act; by 1935, most states were granting cash assistance to widows.

While mothers' aid programs established the principle that single women with dependent children were entitled to public assistance, they did not provide unconditional aid, nor were all women approved for aid. "Suitable home" requirements restricted eligibility to those considered, after investigation, "physically, mentally, and morally fit" to raise their children. Because of racial segregation and prejudice, black families were routinely denied aid and, given the prevailing moral standards, the majority of recipients were widows, not unmarried, separated, or divorced women. Although the assistance was meager and conditional, the aid given to mothers finally broke the prohibitions against home relief, established the state's obligation to help this category of poor, and laid the foundation for our current program, Aid to Families with Dependent Children.

The Great Depression and the New Deal. The Great Depression, which began when the stock market collapsed in 1929 and continued until the late 1930s, caused widespread suffering and destitution. Thirteen to fifteen million Americans lost their jobs, numerous banks failed, and soup kitchens and bread lines to feed the newly poor became common sights throughout the country. No state or federal program existed at this time to help relieve the suffering of these newly poor. In spite of widespread and urgent need, President Herbert Hoover opposed federal intervention, maintaining that government relief to the needy would become the "master of their souls and thoughts."[4]

In the fall of 1932, Franklin Delano Roosevelt was elected president. A man with strong convictions about the government's responsibility to its citizens and bold plans to relieve their suffering, he had enacted the country's first unemployment insurance law while governor of New York. As president, Roosevelt embraced the principle that unemployment, sickness, and old age were conditions beyond the control of individuals, and that providing security and protection against economic hardship was an essential function of the government as well as a right of citizenship. He stated: "If, as our Constitution tells us, our federal government was established among other things 'to promote the general welfare,' it is our plain duty to provide for that security upon which welfare depends."[5]

Although his administration initially responded to the immediate crisis by giving money to the states for poor relief, Roosevelt quickly replaced cash assistance with a massive public jobs initiative for the able-bodied unemployed. "Continued dependence upon relief induces a spiritual and moral disintegration fundamentally destructive to the national fiber," the president warned. "To dole out relief in this way is to administer a narcotic, a subtle destroyer of the human spirit."[6]

The Social Security Act of 1935. On August 14, 1935, President Roosevelt signed the Social Security Act (SSA). With a stroke of the pen, he reversed three centuries of the colonial poor law tradition. For the first time in our history, the federal government acknowledged that it was responsible for the well-being and se-

*President Franklin Delano Roosevelt
signs the landmark Social Security Act
on August 14, 1935.*

curity of its citizens, and that Americans were entitled to this security by virtue of their citizenship.

The Social Security Act and its subsequent amendments created numerous social insurance programs, also known as entitlements, that were designed to prevent Americans from falling into poverty. The programs included Old Age, Disability, and Survivors Insurance for several categories of elderly citizens, Unemployment Insurance for workers who lost their jobs, and Workmen's Compensation for workers who were injured on the job.

Aid to Dependent Children. This historic legislation also created several state and federal public assistance programs for needy Americans who could not work, including the blind, the elderly, and the disabled. Title IV of the act created Aid to Dependent Children (ADC), which provided matching federal money to help states fund mothers' aid programs. Title IV stipulated that children were eligible for benefits if they were "deprived of parental support or care because of a parent's death, absence, or incapacity."

States were given wide discretion in determining who was eligible for ADC and how much they received. In 1939, for instance, Arkansas provided an average of $8.10 a month to eligible families, while Massachusetts provided $61.07. Such variations in payments from state to state remain true today.

Congress allowed each state to maintain "suitable home rules" as well as to "impose such other requirements as to means, moral character, etc. as it sees fit."[7] One such restriction was known as the "man-in-the-house" rule: The presence of a man in the home, including a boarder, visitor, or any unrelated man, automatically made a home unsuitable. Unannounced visits, including evening "raids" by social workers looking for male visitors, were common until the Supreme Court outlawed such practices in the late 1960s.

Although created as an entitlement, ADC was nevertheless considered charity by many, and, unlike the elderly or disabled, whose benefits were provided without scrutiny, its recipients were often subjected to humiliating investigations and looked down on for their need. One social worker recorded the admonishment she gave a client: "Explained that when she accepted charity, she gave up right to make any decisions."[8]

In 1939, Congress made widows with children eligible for Social Security benefits if their husbands had contributed to the system. Because many widows took advantage of the increased benefit level offered by Social Security, ADC gradually supported more divorced, deserted, and, especially after the 1960s, never-married mothers with children. When, in 1950, Congress added a monthly grant for mothers, the program's name was changed to Aid to Families with Dependent Children (AFDC).

Over the course of the next two decades, many programs that extended aid and services to a variety of Americans, including veterans, children, and disabled people, were added to our social welfare system. In 1953, the Department of Health, Education and Welfare was created to oversee this burgeoning system. (This agency is now called the Department of Health and Human Services.)

The Welfare Explosion: 1960 to 1973. While existing social welfare programs were aimed at preventing certain groups of Americans from falling into poverty, they did not raise the standard of living or provide economic or educational opportunities to those who were already poor. Racial segregation and discrimination prevented African Americans, many of whom were now living in northern cities, from acquiring equal education and employment. Many rural residents, especially throughout the South and in the Appalachian region, lived in desperate poverty. Some experts estimated that between 40 and 50 million Americans were without adequate food, shelter, employment, and medical care.

When John F. Kennedy was sworn in as president in 1961, he advised the American people that the "hand of hope must be extended to the poor and depressed."[9] For the next decade and a half, that helping hand came in the form of massive social legislation designed to correct racial, educational, and income inequality. Most of the new measures and expansions of existing programs, however, had little to do with cash assistance to the needy. As President Lyndon Johnson said when he launched his "unconditional" war on poverty in 1964, "Our war on poverty seeks to give the desperate and the downtrodden the skills and experience that they need to lift themselves out of poverty."[10]

"A hand up, not a hand-out" was the intent of the wide array of programs created under the Economic Opportunity Act of 1964, including VISTA, the JOBS Corps, Upward Bound, Neighborhood Youth Corps, and Operation Head Start. These were antipoverty measures; they provided training and educational opportunities and were intended to help the disadvantaged move out of poverty and into the workforce.

During this time, Congress also created several programs designed to improve nutrition and health. The Food Stamp Act replaced surplus food with food vouchers for low-income people; the Medicare amendments to the Social Security Act provided medical services to the

Children with their teacher at a Head Start center in San Diego, California. This federally funded program provides meals for about 600,000 poor children and teaches basic educational and social skills.

elderly; and the Medicaid amendments provided medical care to low-income individuals and families.

Although the federal government did not specifically alter AFDC, it did create a virtual army of advocates for the poor who helped eligible people receive AFDC benefits; many of these people had been unaware of the program, and others had been denied aid. Federally funded legal aid attorneys attacked restrictive welfare policies—such as residency requirements and man-in-the-house rules—in courts at the state and federal level and represented recipients and applicants in disputes with their local welfare offices. Community Action Program workers distributed information about benefits and helped applicants complete the required paperwork; and welfare recipients and community activists joined together to make services known and available to people in need. The National Welfare Rights Organization worked to remove the stigma attached to welfare recipients in favor of dignity and acceptance. Welfare, they believed, was as much a right of citizenship as were social insurance programs.

In response to pressure from the community, which often included demonstrations at local offices, welfare administrators and workers were forced to become more accountable. Welfare recipients were given the right to due process so that eligibility was no longer at the discretion of welfare social workers. As a result of these changes, the number of recipients approved for public assistance went from only 33 percent in 1960 to 90 percent in 1971. During the same period of time, the number of AFDC recipients tripled, from about 745,000 in 1960 to about 3 million by 1972.

When Richard Nixon was elected president in 1968, many assumed that, as a conservative Republican, he would curtail federal spending for antipoverty programs.

During his administration, however, spending for both social insurance and means-tested programs was more than double the amount spent during Johnson's term. Among the many far-reaching initiatives undertaken during his presidency were the establishment of national guidelines for, and the expansion of, the Food Stamp Program; the creation of Supplementary Security Income (SSI), which combined and federalized existing programs for the blind, elderly, and disabled; and the establishment of automatic cost-of-living allowances (COLAs) for SSI and Social Security recipients.

Cultural Changes. From 1960 to 1973, our welfare system grew tremendously as lawmakers expanded social insurance benefits and created many new programs for those who were poor and disadvantaged. In 1965, total state and federal expenditures for all social welfare programs equaled about $142 billion; by 1975, the amount had risen to about $500 billion. Social insurance programs accounted for most of the growth in spending, but spending also doubled for means-tested programs, reaching about $161 billion by 1978. Most of this money went to fund in-kind benefits, including Medicaid, Food Stamps, and educational and job training programs. Although AFDC accounted for only about 10 percent of means-tested spending, this program tripled in size, both in the number of recipients and in costs. Many experts attributed this growth to the relaxation of eligibility requirements, arguing that most of the new recipients had always been eligible for aid.

Another factor that contributed to the rise in welfare dependency during this time was the remarkable increase in the number of single-parent families. Beginning in the mid-1960s, our society began loosening its prohibitions against divorce and premarital sex. As a result, many men and women—rich and poor, black and white—no longer felt obligated to remain in unhappy marriages or to marry if they had a child. Although this phenomenon cut across racial and economic lines, African-American families experienced the most dramatic change in family composition. By 1965, one out of four black children lived in female-headed households. By 1994, this number had risen to two out of three.

These changing attitudes led many women to put their energy and talents into work outside the home. Less educated and skilled women, however, were hard-pressed to find jobs that adequately supported themselves and their children. In addition, as mothers freed themselves from the obligation of marriage, many fathers freed themselves from the obligation of child support. As a result, many single mothers found themselves poor and dependent on public assistance.

Although the programs created to alleviate the suffering of the poor did not wipe out poverty in America, they did improve the quality of life for many poor people. Expansion of the Food Stamp program helped feed millions of hungry people; expansion of Medicaid provided crucial medical insurance for poor children and adults; and SSI provided a guaranteed annual income for low-income aged, blind, and disabled people. Despite measurable improvements, these programs had many critics. Pointing to increasing numbers of welfare-dependent mothers, some experts charged that our welfare system encouraged a culture of poverty and dependency rather than self-improvement and independence.

After forty years of expansion, and despite growing suspicions that there were flaws that needed correction, our welfare system enjoyed broad support from both citizens and lawmakers. Most people still supported the basic principle that our government had a fundamental responsibility to improve the welfare of all its citizens, including the poor.

Retreat. The first limits were put on our welfare system when Ronald Reagan was elected president in 1980. A staunch conservative, Reagan believed that government intervention impeded the economic and social growth of the country. Harking back to nineteenth-century values of rugged individualism, competition, and a free-market economy, Reagan promised to cut taxes, reduce domestic spending, and rid the welfare rolls of "cheats and freeloaders." Citing two decades of expansion, he believed that it was time to remove all but the "truly needy" from assistance.

The push to reduce government spending came both as a result of ideology and as a reaction to the economy, which had begun to falter. Beginning in the mid-1970s, the country experienced high inflation and unemployment, as well as a steep decline in wages for working people. Manufacturing jobs began to disappear, especially in cities, and were replaced in great part by lower-paying service jobs. Unemployment rates began to increase in urban areas, and poverty rates, which had declined significantly until the mid-1970s, reached a high for the decade in 1983. For those who survived on welfare payments, times were never worse. Unlike Social Security, AFDC benefits were not adjusted for increases in the cost of living. As a result, the value of these benefits began to decline.

Despite President Reagan's desire to reduce the size of government during his two administrations, spending for social insurance programs increased and, as the number of poor rose, spending for AFDC was actually as high when he left office in 1988 as it had been when he entered. To the dismay of many, he did reduce federal spending for numerous domestic programs that helped low-income people. Cuts in Medicaid, school lunch programs, Head Start, Food Stamps, day care, child nutrition, family planning, and youth employment programs came to about $2 billion a year during the eight years Reagan was in office. Millions of low-income families were affected. Urban areas were especially hard hit. While in 1980 nearly $24 billion in federal money helped states fund community development, job and training programs, and housing assistance, by 1988 this amount had been cut to $13 billion. At the same time, the Reagan administration granted tax breaks to the richest Americans, further widening the gap between the rich and the poor. In other words, the rich became richer, and the poor became poorer.

Some experts claimed that the government, by withdrawing vital services and resources for health, education, and employment, contributed directly to the increase in poverty, especially for people of color in urban areas. Other analysts argued that the poor needed to take more responsibility for changing their situation and to depend less on the government.

Many legislators believed that the welfare system was in need of major reform. Although Democrats and Republicans had fundamentally different approaches to social policy, together they formulated a plan that they hoped would reduce welfare dependency and help recipients become self-supporting. The Family Support Act of 1988 was the result of this bipartisan effort. Regarded by many as a new social contract between recipients and government, the act demands work obligations from recipients and financial obligations from absent fathers; and increases educational and job training, child care, and medical services and support from the government.

Throughout the 1980s, and through the administration of President George Bush, poverty became more severe and chronic, especially in urban areas. Welfare dependency worsened; and high unemployment, the drug trade, and crime accelerated the decline of our cities. In 1991, forty states froze or cut benefits to AFDC recipients, and many began linking behavioral requirements to benefits. When Los Angeles exploded in violence in 1992, many people were not surprised. President Bush, they claimed, had largely ignored the plight of the poor during his presidency.

Although support for the numerous protections that our social welfare system affords so many Americans remains high, dissatisfaction with programs designed to help the poor has grown. Are we spending too much money on programs that return too little? How much money should we spend on social insurance programs compared with those that help low-income people? Who benefits the most from social welfare programs? What are the requirements for welfare programs and what do they provide?

Our Current
System

Most Americans benefit in some way from our system of social welfare. The retired person who collects Social Security checks, the low-income family who receives Food Stamps, the college student who is granted a low-interest federal college loan, the worker who collects unemployment after losing a factory job, the child who attends Head Start, and the single woman who receives Aid to Families with Dependent Children are all beneficiaries of our system of social welfare.

Composed of more than two hundred federal and state programs, the system is a complex patchwork of social insurance and means-tested programs and includes cash assistance and noncash, or in-kind, benefits. In 1992, total expenditures for all of these programs amounted to about $711 billion. More than two thirds of this money was spent on only three programs: Social Security, Medicaid, and Medicare, accounting for $285 billion, $129 billion, and $68 billion, respectively.[1]

Social Insurance Programs. Social insurance programs include Old Age, Survivors, and Disability Insurance (collectively known as Social Security), Unemployment Insurance, Workers' Compensation, Military Retirement and Disability, Other Nonmilitary Retirement and Disability Benefits (public employee pensions), Medicare, and smaller programs that target other special categories. In 1992, federal and state expenditures for these programs totaled about $545 billion.

Social insurance programs are contributory programs—that is, individuals or, in the case of unemployment compensation, employers pay into the system through payroll deductions. Benefit levels are determined by how much an individual earned during a certain period or lifetime of employment. The more an individual earns, the more he or she is given back. The amount a recipient ultimately receives, however, may be greater than the amount he or she actually contributed. Most retirees, for example, receive benefits that total two to five times more than their contributions. After about seven years, benefits actually come from taxes collected from current workers.

Social Security provides cash assistance to retired citizens who are sixty-two years of age or older, survivors of deceased workers, and those forced to retire because of disability. Beneficiaries are granted cost-of-living increases each year. In 1991, the federal government allowed an individual to receive a maximum of $1,022 a month. The average Social Security pension for a worker who retired at age sixty-five, however, amounted to about $602 a month.

Medicare provides limited medical coverage to elderly citizens. Beneficiaries commonly contribute to the cost of this insurance, and because the services it provides are limited, many people must purchase additional medical insurance. This program accounts for about 22 percent of all social insurance costs. Both Social Security and Medicare are federal programs overseen by the Social Security Administration.

Unemployment Insurance is available to workers who are involuntarily unemployed. Workers who quit or are fired from their jobs for misconduct, or who refuse employment, are not eligible for unemployment compensation. Benefits are based on a percentage of past earnings and are funded through an employers' payroll tax. Most of this money is returned to the states to administer the program. Although the maximum duration of benefits for an unemployed person is usually twenty-six weeks, a state may extend this coverage if its unemployment rate exceeds a certain percentage. The amount a worker may collect depends on the salary earned, but a maximum weekly amount is fixed by each state. These maximums range from about $100 to $300 a week. In 1992, $37 billion was spent in funding this program.

Means-tested Programs. The goal of social insurance programs is to help individuals and families "maintain the security they have achieved through productive work."[2] These programs are considered by society as "rewards for work," and at some point in their lives, most Americans will probably enjoy the benefits and protections they offer.

Extensive as they are, these programs do not protect everyone, nor do they adequately defend against other misfortunes that people may experience in their lives. Many elderly and disabled people haven't had enough work experience to qualify for Social Security. Fewer than half of unemployed workers qualify for unemployment insurance. Many working people are unable to

This man has come to an unemployment office in Brooklyn, New York. He has to ask for help in reading about benefits because he is illiterate. Some studies estimate that as many as *12* percent of American adults cannot read.

make ends meet because their wages are too low. And millions of single parents do not have sufficient income or child support payments to support their children.

There are a variety of programs available that provide economic assistance and opportunity to low-income Americans. Unlike social insurance programs, which base eligibility and benefit levels largely on past earnings, these programs are income-tested or means-tested, that is, they base eligibility on financial need. In order to qualify for this kind of help, a household's income must fall below a certain level. For most means-tested programs, a household's total assets, including money in the bank, must also fall below a specific level.

In-kind Benefits. Most of the help available to poor people is in the form of in-kind benefits, not cash assistance. Some programs aim to improve the quality of life of those without enough money for food, shelter, medical care, or education. These include food subsidies such as the Food Stamp Program, the School Lunch Program, and the Women and Child Nutrition Program; medical insurance or Medicaid; housing subsidies, which provide public housing or vouchers toward rental assistance; and Low-Income Home Energy Assistance, which helps needy families pay their energy costs.

Medicaid is a state and federal program that provides medical insurance to low-income Americans. Because each state, within the broad guidelines of the federal government, administers its own program, Medicaid benefits and eligibility requirements vary widely.

Many low-income people are automatically eligible for Medicaid, including those who receive SSI and AFDC. For other low-income people, household income and other available resources must fall below a certain level in order for them to qualify. Medicaid currently provides medical insurance to more than 24 million people. Federal and state expenditures for this program are projected to be more than $250 billion by the year 2000.

The Food Stamp Program provides coupons, which are redeemable for food at retail stores, to low-income individuals and families. Like Medicaid, certain categories of needy Americans, such as SSI and AFDC recipients, are automatically eligible for food stamps. The amount of stamps a family receives depends upon both its size and its income. A family of four with no income receives about $350 a month in food stamps. A household with income must meet specific income and resource standards after deducting costs for child care, excess shelter costs, medical expenses, and a percentage of earned income. Families, for instance, may not have more than $2,000 in disposable assets available to them, and their net income after deductions must not exceed 100 percent of the poverty line.

Recipients must apply at least once a year and must report income changes of $25 or more. A parent whose child is over the age of twelve must register for work. People who live in group homes, including homeless shelters, battered women's shelters, and nursing homes, are allowed to use their food stamps to purchase meals prepared by nonprofit agencies. At the national level, the program is administered by the Food and Nutrition Service of the Department of Agriculture, and state welfare agencies and district Social Security offices administer the program locally. More than 25 million people a year receive food stamps at a cost of about $23 billion.

A group of other means-tested programs, sometimes called "antipoverty" measures, aim to improve the *future* economic condition of disadvantaged individuals

A mother fills in forms to apply for food stamps while her three children color a picture together.

through job training and education. Head Start, an educational program for economically disadvantaged preschool children, and the Job Corps, a training program for those with no or few job skills, are examples of this type of government-funded program.

Among the more than seventy means-tested programs in current operation are special programs that help specific categories of needy Americans, including the homeless, needy veterans, foster grandparents, adoptive parents, black lung sufferers, refugees, and migrant workers. In 1991, the total cost of means-tested programs was about $210 billion: two thirds of this was spent on in-kind benefits.

Income Support Programs. Supplemental Security Income, Aid to Families with Dependent Children, and General Assistance are cash assistance or income support programs designed to provide a "safety net" against complete destitution for people who, for a variety of reasons, are unable to or are not expected to meet their own financial needs.

Supplemental Security Income (SSI) is a federally funded and administered program that provides monthly cash assistance and medical benefits to approximately 5 million low-income elderly, blind, and disabled people. Eligibility requirements and grant amounts are the same in all states. A recipient must have an income of less than about $5,000 a year and must meet specific standards regarding age, disability, or visual acuity. Appropriate state agencies determine if a medical disability exists, and Social Security Administration district offices examine the applicant's documentation and process the application.

The maximum amount of $422 a month is available to individuals who live in their own households; $633 a month is available to couples who both qualify. Recipients receive automatic cost-of-living increases and, in all but two states, may also qualify for additional state supplements. Approximately 5 million Americans receive SSI benefits. The overwhelming majority are aged or disabled; only about 84,000 are blind. Because they are elderly or disabled, SSI recipients are not expected or required to work, but, in an effort to encourage work experience and independent living, they are allowed to earn a certain amount of money each month without losing all their benefits. If disqualified for benefits because of earnings, a recipient is very often able to retain Medicaid benefits. Additionally, the Employment Opportunities for Disabled Americans Act of 1986 grants special benefits and Medicaid to recipients whose earned income makes them ineligible for SSI. The federal government spent about $18 billion in SSI benefits in 1992, and state-administered supplements amounted to an additional $500 million.

General Assistance is an optional state assistance program for indigent unemployed individuals who do not qualify for other social welfare programs. The average monthly grant is less than $200. Neither disabled, aged, nor responsible for dependent children, this category of welfare recipients is usually considered by the larger society to be "able-bodied." Many states, citing budget restraints and public reluctance to support the able-bodied poor, have eliminated or curtailed General Assistance programs. In 1993, approximately 1.3 million people received this kind of assistance at a cost of about $3 billion.

The *Earned-Income Tax Credit (EITC)* is one of the few government programs designed to raise the income level of poor working families with children. Administered by the Internal Revenue Service, the EITC helps to supplement the low wages of working families with children by reducing the amount of taxes a family owes the government. If the credit is larger than the taxes owed, the government pays the family the difference. Families with incomes below $23,070 are eligible for this tax credit. A maximum credit of $1,513 is available to families with two children who earn between $7,760 and $12,210. Those who earn either less or more than this range receive a partial credit. In 1993, about 13.7 million people received an average of about $872 through this credit at a cost to the government of about $11 billion. President Bill Clinton has recommended that this program be expanded to more working poor families.

Aid to Families with Dependent Children (AFDC), the program most people associate with "welfare," supports needy single parents with dependent children. Federal and state governments share the cost of the program. The Administration for Children and Families, an agency within the U.S. Department of Health and Human Services, establishes basic guidelines and requirements; state governments determine benefit levels, formulate other eligibility requirements, and administer their own programs.

States employ a formula to determine the income eligibility of a family: Gross income of the household cannot exceed 185 percent of the state's needs standard—the minimum amount required to meet basic living expenses in that particular state—after disregarding certain income. These "disregards" include the first $50 per month of child support, some work and child care expenses, and a certain amount of earned income. The Family Support Act (discussed in detail in Chapter 6) provides additional work incentives, supportive services, and educational opportunities for recipients as well as work and educational requirements. These services and requirements are intended to encourage recipients to enter the workforce, increase their earnings and potential, and become self-supporting.

Although approximately 88 percent of AFDC recipients are single women, some two-parent families are also eligible for aid. Aid to Families with Dependent Children-Unemployed Parent (AFDC-UP) helps support two-parent families if the principal earner—the parent who earned the greater income during the previous twenty-four months—is unemployed. This parent must have worked a specified amount of time or have received unemployment within one year of applying for aid. There are several ways in which the earner can establish the required work time, including participation in educational or job training programs. Of the 4.9 million families who received AFDC in 1993, only 359,016 of them received AFDC-UP benefits.

Each state determines the amount of money a family can receive. Adjusted to the size of the family, this amount is based on a percentage of the state's needs standard. In Mississippi, for instance, a family of three received a monthly grant of $120 in May 1994; in Connecticut, the grant for the same size family was $581. The average AFDC monthly grant is about $375. Because of their very low income, AFDC recipients are automatically eligible for food stamps and Medicaid, and may apply for housing assistance, low-interest educational loans, and other means-tested benefits.

Unlike Social Security or SSI, states do not give AFDC users automatic cost-of-living increases. As a result, the actual value of benefits has fallen by about 42 percent since 1970.[3] In addition, many states have frozen or reduced the amount of their grants to families. In 1993, more than 14 million people living in nearly 5 million families received AFDC, representing an increase of about 33 percent since 1989. Expenditures for AFDC from both federal and state governments currently amount to about $23 billion a year.

The New Paternalism. Although many AFDC recipients are divorced or legally separated women, more than half have never been married. As the percentage of young, unwed mothers receiving AFDC has increased, long-term dependency has risen as well. Many states are trying to reduce welfare rolls and long-term dependency by modifying the behavior of AFDC clients. Under a system known as the "new paternalism," states are now, through a variety of rewards and penalties such as bonuses, reductions, or terminations, attaching an array of specific behavioral requirements to welfare eligibility.

Some states propose to reduce benefits if an AFDC client has another child while on welfare, if she doesn't bring her child for regular doctor's visits, or if her child does not attend school regularly. Some have recommended that a cash bonus be given to unwed mothers who marry the father of their dependent child or who voluntarily use birth control to limit the size of their families.

While these policies are becoming more common—especially as state budgets become tighter, taxpayers less generous, and inner cities more disordered—they remain very controversial. One source of controversy concerns the right of the government to manage the personal conduct of one specific group of people—AFDC recipients.

Supporters of these new policies argue that if the government is paying for services, it has a right to demand that welfare recipients adopt certain behaviors—delaying childbirth, staying in school, securing employment, and adequately caring for their dependent children—that they believe are related to economic wellbeing. Critics, however, claim that these rules not only punish poor people but are ineffective methods of addressing the root causes of poverty and welfare dependency. According to analysts, these underlying causes include economic conditions, unequal distribution of wealth, racial and gender discrimination, and an inadequate social welfare system.

Are people poor because they do not work or do not try hard enough to work? Are they poor because they are denied the opportunities that more affluent people have available to them? How effective is our system of welfare in lifting the disadvantaged, the vulnerable, and the poor out of poverty?

Poverty
in America

With a median family income of $31,900 and a gross national product of $5.9 trillion, the United States is one of the richest countries in the world. Our democratic system of government and free-market economy have the potential to provide all citizens an equal opportunity to live a decent and productive life. Despite an abundance of wealth and resources, individual and economic freedom, and a high standard of living, millions of Americans live in poverty.

In 1992, according to the U.S. Bureau of the Census, approximately 37 million Americans, or 14.7 percent of the population, had incomes so low that the government classified them as "officially poor." This is the highest number of people living in poverty since 1964—the year President Lyndon Johnson initiated his famous War on Poverty. Record numbers of Americans are receiving food stamps and/or collecting AFDC, and shelters and soup kitchens are housing and feeding countless needy and hungry families. While most Americans who

Millions of American children — one in five — grow up trapped by poverty.

become poor move out of poverty within two years, a small but growing percentage do not escape this condition, remaining trapped in chronic poverty for many years—even generations.

Measuring Poverty. As alarming as the figures are, many experts believe that poverty is even more widespread and severe than government estimates indicate. The United States Bureau of the Census measures what is known as absolute poverty, or the inability to purchase the basic goods and services needed to survive. Absolute poverty means not having enough to eat every day, not having adequate shelter or clothing, and not having access to medical care. The government determines the minimum amount of money needed to purchase these basic necessities; if a household has an annual income that falls below this fixed amount, it is said to be living below the poverty line, or poverty threshold. The government does not count noncash benefits such as food stamps or Medicaid as income.

The poverty line varies according to family size and composition (single parent or two-parent) and is adjusted each year to account for changes in consumer prices. In 1970, a family of four was considered poor if its income was below $3,968; in 1980, $8,414; and in 1993, $14,335.

Since its creation in 1963, the official poverty line has been a source of controversy. Many people believe that the way the government calculates this threshold is obsolete. The formula assumes that—as was the case in the 1960s—the average family spends about one third of its budget on food and the rest to pay for housing, transportation, clothing, health care, and other basic necessities. Using that ratio, the government figures the minimum amount that a family needs to survive by multiplying the cost of purchasing an "economy food plan," as defined by the U.S. Department of Agriculture, by three. Many poverty experts believe that this formula should be revised to reflect the changes in the cost of living and the spending habits of average Americans. As housing and energy costs have risen over the last several decades, most families are spending more of their income to pay for housing, energy, and transportation; they spend only about one fifth of their incomes on food. If the cost of food were multiplied by five instead of three, the poverty threshold would be almost twice the current level; millions more people would then fall below the new poverty line and would be eligible for government assistance.

According to Gallup polls conducted over the past two decades, most Americans agree that the current poverty line is too low. Only those who had incomes of 150 percent of the official poverty line said that they were able to afford adequate food, clothing, medical care, and shelter for their families throughout the year.[1]

John E. Schwarz and Thomas J. Volgy, political scientists and authors of *The Forgotten Americans,* believe that a family of four needs at least $21,600 just to purchase the basic necessities. These authors describe the hardships that one hard-working family experiences, despite an income above the poverty line. Both high school graduates, Bruce and Sara Lanier (whose names were changed to protect their privacy) are raising twin daughters. Bruce works full-time as a carpenter and Sara works part-time as a sales clerk. Because their combined income is $19,700, the government does not count them as being poor. Their life, however, is filled with deprivation:

*They cannot afford a telephone, and most months there
are times when they either skip meals or must "borrow"
from relatives or friends to pay for food. They walk several miles each way to work when they have too little
money to fix their fourteen-year-old car. They have no
medical insurance and the twins have never been to a
dentist. When they cannot pay their utility bills, their
heat is turned off, sometimes in the cold of winter.*[2]

Relative Poverty. Poverty is not only the inability to
purchase life's most basic necessities, it is also the inability to participate in the normal activities of society.
While absolute poverty calculates the minimum income
required to attain the basic necessities needed to survive
in a society, relative poverty measures how one's income compares with the income or standard of living of
others. Poverty in America, for instance, is often less
severe, chronic, and widespread than poverty in devel-
oping countries. Poverty is relative within a country as
well. British economist Peter Townsend defines relative
poverty as "the lack of resources necessary to permit
participation in the activities, customs, and diet commonly approved by society."[3]

In the United States, many poor and low-income
families are unable to enjoy the activities that the average American takes for granted: taking a family trip or
vacation; going to a movie or out to dinner; or owning
a telephone, a car, or a home. A person's life is also
impoverished when the community lacks clean and safe
streets or parks; adequate schools; or sufficient police,
fire, or medical services.

There are some analysts, on the other hand, who
argue that the government overestimates poverty because the cash value of food stamps, Medicaid, and
other benefits are not counted as income. Adding the

cash value of these benefits would push a significant number of people over the poverty line. Robert Rector, an analyst with the Heritage Foundation, a conservative research agency, believes that only a "tiny percentage of Americans" are truly deprived of life's basic necessities, arguing that most poor people today experience a higher standard of living than ever before.[4] In response to dissatisfaction with the current method used to calculate poverty, Congress has authorized a panel of experts from the National Academy of Sciences to examine the issue. Patricia Ruggles, an economist with the Urban Institute, predicts that if the panel does recommend changing the poverty line, the most likely result will be that the poverty line is raised by about 50 percent, "substantially increasing the number of people regarded as poor."[5]

The Consequences of Poverty. For the millions of Americans currently left out of the American dream of opportunity and prosperity, life is filled with hardship and deprivation as well as depression and hopelessness. The poor in America experience hunger, physical and mental illness, infant mortality, school failure, family dissolution, teen pregnancy, crime, and substance abuse at twice or more the rates of the nonpoor.

The vicious circle of chronic poverty, often passed from generation to generation, robs children and their families of their potential to participate in the rich social and economic opportunities and activities available in the United States. In 1964, the Economic Report to the President described poverty in this way:

Low incomes carry with them high risks of illness; limitations on mobility; limited access to education, information, and training. Poor parents can't give their chil-

*A homeless family, headed by a single
mother, in a Philadelphia shelter.*

dren the opportunity for better health and education needed to improve their lot . . . Thus the cruel legacy of poverty is passed from parents to their children." [6]

Who Are the Poor? Our free-market system of economy holds out the possibility of economic prosperity for all, but it does not guarantee economic security to any citizen. Recessions, depressions, inflation, changing job markets, low wages, and even natural disasters are factors that can adversely affect any American family's financial situation. While these events can affect anyone at any time, some Americans experience poverty more frequently and for longer periods than does the general population. The following statistics, projected from the U.S. Census Bureau's 1991 Current Population Survey, illustrate the impact that age, race, work effort, and family composition have on economic status.

Family Composition. More than half of all poor Americans, or 54 percent, live in families headed by a single mother—a poverty rate triple that of two-parent families. There are several reasons why single parents are so vulnerable to poverty.

First, there is only one income to support the whole family. In the majority of two-parent families, either both parents work full-time or one works full-time and the other works part-time.

Second, women are generally paid less money than men, so that even if a single mother works full-time, her salary is often insufficient for her family's needs. If she left school to have children, or has little work experience, she is liable to qualify only for very low-paying jobs. If she has young children, the cost of child care further erodes her income. Single parents who receive

AFDC remain poor because the monthly grants they receive are so low.

Third, a single parent usually does not receive adequate child support from the child's father to make up for the loss of his income to the family. In fact, the majority of divorced single parents receive no child support at all, and unwed parents are even less likely to receive payments. (An in-depth discussion of family composition, poverty, and welfare dependence is presented in Chapter 5.)

Age. While about 10 percent of the country's poor are elderly, a full 40 percent are children under eighteen. Today, one in five children in America is poor—the highest U.S. child poverty rate since 1965, and the highest child poverty rate among industrialized countries. Minority children, who compose about one third of the American children under the age of six, accounted for almost two thirds of all the poor children in that age category.

The consequences of child poverty are well-known:

From the womb to adulthood, poor children are at higher risk of health, developmental, and educational setbacks—problems that are likely to follow them through life. For some children, poverty is deadly. Each year, an estimated 10,000 children die from poverty's effects. For many more, poverty leads to inadequate health care, hunger, family stress, inability to concentrate in the classroom, and school drop out.[7]

These are conditions that can defeat the spirit, causing many impoverished citizens to become passive, depressed, and despondent. Trapped in deprivation and hardship, some families become so overwhelmed that they are unable to provide the structure, guidance, and nurturing that their children need. Although by no means restricted to low-income families, child abuse and neglect often stem from the stress and isolation that poor families experience.

Race. Despite dramatic and significant advances for minority groups in all spheres of American life, especially since the mid-1960s, many barriers still exist that prevent full economic, educational, and social equality. As a result, although non-Hispanic whites compose almost half of all poor Americans, minorities experience disproportionately high rates of poverty. About 11 percent of white Americans were poor in 1991, compared with 32.7 percent of African Americans and 28.7 percent of Hispanics.

In addition to low-paying jobs and high rates of unemployment, family structure is a significant factor in these high rates of poverty. The majority of black families are now headed by single women; about two out of three black children are born to mothers who have never been married.

Native Americans experience the highest rates of poverty in America. More than half of approximately 3 million American Indians have incomes below the poverty line; 44 percent are unemployed; 21 percent have no indoor plumbing; and 16 percent have no electricity. They have the highest infant mortality rate in the country, the highest rate of fetal alcohol syndrome in the world, and the lowest life expectancy rate—one in three Native Americans will die before reaching the age of forty-five, twenty years sooner than any one else in America.[8]

A grandmother keeps an eye on her grandchildren from her window as they walk to school in the drug-infested, crime-ridden neighborhood of the South Bronx, New York.

Chronic Poverty. The "poorest of the poor," "the truly disadvantaged," and "the underclass" are terms often used to describe a minority of poor Americans for whom poverty has become a permanent condition. Composed primarily of urban blacks and Hispanics, the persistently poor often live in ghettos wracked by extreme poverty, decay, and disorder. Many experts believe that the problems that plague these neighborhoods—drugs, alcoholism, crime, domestic violence, gangs, illegitimacy, soaring high-school dropout rates— attest to the consequences of racial, social, and economic isolation.

This kind of poverty, explains William Julius Wilson, professor of sociology at the University of Chicago, is in part a result of dramatic economic changes that occurred when intense foreign competition in the production of goods reduced the number and kinds of manufacturing jobs available in the United States. The loss of more than 2 million jobs in the textile, automobile, coal, and steel industries, and the shift to lower-paying service and higher-skilled information processing or high-technology jobs, have been devastating for working-class residents in both urban and rural areas.

When jobs started disappearing from our cities, and chronic unemployment, crime, drugs, and gangs began to increase, stable working-class and middle-class families in the black community left these neighborhoods. As a result, Wilson explains:

Today's ghetto neighborhoods are populated almost exclusively by the most disadvantaged segments of the black urban community; that heterogeneous grouping of families and individuals who are outside the mainstream of the American economic system. Included in this group are individuals who lack training and skills and either experience long-term unemployment or are not members of the labor force, individuals who are engaged in street crime and other forms of aberrant behavior, and families that experience long-term spells of poverty and/or welfare dependency. These are the populations to which I refer when I speak of the underclass.[9]

Some analysts believe that cultural factors are as much to blame for chronic poverty as economic ones. The development of a permanently poor class of Americans, says conservative author Lawrence Mead, is a result of a decline in moral standards, low work effort (not lack of opportunity), and the development of a "culture of poverty." Within that culture, employment, family planning, and responsibility are spurned. He claims that it is the "failure of most poor adults to work steadily in *any* job, not the inferiority of their positions, that largely explains their predicament."[10]

Rural Poverty. Chronic poverty is not only an urban phenomenon: Severe and long-term poverty plagues rural areas as well. In fact, studies show that while they are fewer in number, the rural poor experience unemployment, inadequate medical care and housing, hunger, and low income at even higher rates than do their urban counterparts.[11] Residents in rural areas are not, for the most part, farmers, but depend on manufacturing for their livelihoods. They are, therefore, equally affected by the general decline that our country has experienced in such industries as steel, coal, and textiles. Migrant workers, who depend on low-paying and seasonal agricultural work, do not have the means to acquire their own land on which to grow food and often spend more than half their meager wages to feed their families and to pay for housing that is often expensive and substandard.

The Working Poor. Poverty rates and unemployment rates are highly correlated: When unemployment increases, the number of poor people increases, and when economic conditions are favorable, poverty rates decline. Employment, however, does not prevent poverty. Many jobs pay so little that even full-time employment still leaves a worker poor. In 1991, according to the Census Bureau, 9 percent of poor Americans were employed full-time and year-round, and about 40 percent worked either part-time or for only part of the year.

Many people believe that these statistics grossly underestimate the number of working Americans who are unable to adequately support their families on their wages. Authors John E. Schwarz and Thomas J. Volgy estimate that nearly 10 million full-time workers live on incomes that are only 150 percent of the poverty line.[12] In addition, employment does not insure all Americans against other hazards. More than 20 million full-time workers do not have health insurance, and about 30 percent of unemployed workers are ineligible for unemployment compensation.

The Causes of Poverty. Experts have debated the root causes of poverty for centuries. Economic trends, unequal distribution of wealth, discrimination, Republican policies, Democratic policies, unequal opportunities, a self-perpetuating culture of poverty, and lack of individual effort are but a few of the many explanations for the existence of "poverty amid plenty" in America. While there are numerous theories that attempt to explain why poverty exists, no single scientific explanation has been accepted by everyone.

In general, liberal thinkers believe that poverty exists because our economic system is flawed: Not enough jobs are created to provide employment for everyone; an unequal distribution of wealth permits some people to become very rich while others live in desperate poverty; and our welfare system does not meet the needs of the poor and disadvantaged. Conservatives, on the other hand, tend to argue that the root of today's poverty lies in individual flaws: low work effort, low educational attainment, passivity, and irresponsible family planning. They further charge that a permissive welfare system encourages these behaviors by rewarding the recipients with cash and other benefits.

While there is considerable disagreement about the root causes of poverty, most people agree that the phenomenal increase in the number of single-parent families has had a significant impact on child poverty and welfare dependency. More than half the poor in America live in mother-only homes. Many work hard to support their families but are still poor. More than 4 million single-parent families are poor because they depend on AFDC for support. How can the government help poor single parents become self-supporting? Can government policies affect family structure? Why are so few single mothers able to count on financial support from their children's fathers? These are a few of the questions that surround the ongoing debate about poverty, family, and welfare.

Welfare and Family Composition

Family Values. During the 1992 presidential campaign, Republican Vice President Dan Quayle told an audience in San Francisco that the "failure of our families is hurting America deeply. . . . Children need mothers and fathers. A welfare check is not a husband. The state is not a father. . . . Bearing babies irresponsibly is, simply, wrong." One example of the breakdown in traditional values, said the vice president, was the decision of a character in a television series to have a child out of wedlock. He stated that this fictional character, a news anchor named Murphy Brown, "'mocked the importance of fathers by bearing a child alone and calling it just another 'lifestyle choice.' "[1]

Although Quayle was widely criticized for his comments regarding single parents, most experts agree that the growth in the number of single-parent families, especially those headed by unwed and teen parents, is indeed cause for alarm. The relationship between single parenthood and poverty, welfare dependency, and the overall decline in the well being of American children are the subjects of considerable discussion and research. Since the 1960s, the percentage of female-headed households has tripled. Half of all marriages now end in divorce, and it is estimated that fewer than half of the children born in 1992 will live their entire childhood with both their biological mother and father. Although the majority of single parents are divorced or separated women, the fastest-growing category of single parents is those who have never been married. Both black and white families have experienced dramatic increases in the percentage of out-of-wedlock births. In 1960, about 25 percent of black children and 6 percent of white children were born to unmarried mothers; by 1994 these rates had risen to nearly 70 percent and 22 percent, respectively.

Teen Parents. An alarming number of single mothers in the United States first became parents as teenagers. In fact, our country has the highest teen pregnancy rate among all industrialized countries. While as recently as twenty years ago most pregnant teens either released their babies for adoption or married the fathers, today about 90 percent of pregnant teens keep their children, and only a minority marry the fathers. And the majority of these young single mothers depend on welfare for support.

If the risks are so great for poverty and hardship, why are so many young women having children without the financial and emotional support of a partner? One factor that may contribute to these high rates is the age at which so many young people are becoming sexually active. Adolescents often engage in risk-taking behavior, and many are simply not mature enough to under-

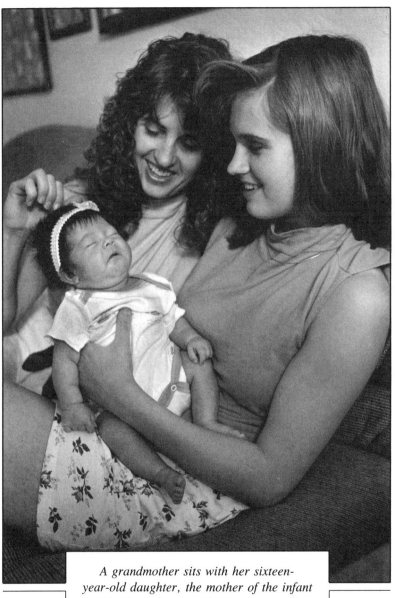

A grandmother sits with her sixteen-year-old daughter, the mother of the infant girl. The father was thirteen years old.

stand the consequences of their actions. Indeed, teen parents commonly blame ignorance about conception and birth control for their pregnancies.

Some young people believe that a baby will give a purpose to their lives. Those who have experienced turmoil, neglect, or disruption in their families often believe that a child will satisfy their own need for love and acceptance.

Joanne (her name has been changed to protect her privacy)—whose father was never involved in her life and whose mother's alcoholism left her unable to provide the nurturing that her daughter needed—always felt unloved and abandoned. She began dating at age thirteen and, looking for the intimacy and acceptance her family had never given her, almost immediately became sexually active. When she became pregnant at age sixteen, she said she was looking forward to being a mother because a baby would love her and never leave her. Although she wanted to give her baby the love she never received, Joanne was totally unprepared for the demands of motherhood. Unfortunately, because she was so emotionally damaged herself, this mother was unable to meet her child's needs. Within two years, despite extensive social services aimed at helping this troubled family, including parenting classes and counseling, Joanne released her child for adoption.

Family Structure and Child Well-being. According to child poverty specialists at the Children's Defense Fund (CDF), the decline in stable, two-parent families has placed children at risk for educational, psychological, and social difficulties. The principal cause of these risks, says CDF director Marian Wright Edelman, is the high rate of poverty that children in single-parent families experience, a rate six times that of intact families.

In addition, the younger the parent, the greater the risk for economic difficulty.

Young single parents, particularly those who were never married, commonly lack adequate education, work experience or training, and do not have the emotional and financial support of a partner. These deficits greatly reduce their ability to achieve economic independence and security. Young single mothers not only experience poverty at higher rates than any other group of single parents, but they do so for longer periods of time. They are the most likely to become long-term welfare recipients; 40 percent of never-married welfare recipients stay on welfare for ten years or longer.[2]

Families and Welfare. The relationship between family composition and welfare dependency is the subject of great debate. According to a survey conducted by David T. Ellwood, author of *Poor Support* and current assistant secretary of the Department of Health and Human Services, more than half of the people surveyed believe that poor women purposely have babies in order to collect welfare benefits. Ironically, respondents who were themselves poor were the most likely to agree.[3] In spite of the fact that welfare recipients have an average of only 1.9 children, a number slightly lower than for the general population, the suspicion persists that AFDC recipients keep having children in order to remain on welfare.

While few experts believe that welfare grants actually entice couples to dissolve their marriages or have children without the benefit of marriage, there are some who believe that our welfare system, by offering cash grants and other benefits to single parents, has contributed to the increase in single-parent families. AFDC, they claim, allows single parents to survive and fathers

A single mother sits with her three-year-old daughter in a Sacramento shelter. She came to California with her three young children in hope of finding a better life than the one she knew in Mississippi.

to abandon their families. Welfare, says one author, "the umbilical cord through which mainstream society sustains the isolated ghetto society, enables the expansion of this single-parent culture. It is its economic life support system."[4]

Most experts, however, believe that welfare itself has little to do with the major transformation of the American family since the 1960s. In fact, states with high benefit levels have no more unwed mothers than states with low benefits. If anything, the reverse is true; states with lower levels of aid actually have slightly higher numbers of out-of-wedlock births. Ellwood claims that "no highly regarded study has indicated that welfare has played more than a minor role in the changing patterns of families overall."[5]

Ellwood is among the majority of welfare experts who argue that cultural and economic factors, rather than the availability of AFDC, largely account for the number of female-headed families.

Social and Cultural Factors. As discussed in Chapter 1, during the 1960s, several social and cultural revolutions transformed the ways that Americans thought about marriage, relationships, child-rearing, and a woman's role in the home and the workplace. The feminist movement, which advocated economic and social equality for women, was instrumental in changing traditional attitudes about sex, marriage, and the family. By the end of the 1960s, the conventional American family—two parents, mother at home, and father at work— was disappearing as women began to enter the workforce in record numbers, had fewer children, and sought economic equality and independence.

Birth control became widely available during this time, giving women sexual and reproductive freedom.

Many men and women strove for individual happiness and freedom and, in the process, rejected the social and religious pressure to marry or stay unhappily married for the sake of the children. Divorce, once frowned upon by society, became more accepted and commonplace.

To some extent, and to the dismay of many Americans, even the stigma of out-of-wedlock pregnancy and parenthood has diminished. Gone are the days when a pregnant teenager was hidden from her neighbors in a home for unwed mothers and the child's birth certificate was stamped ILLEGITIMATE. Gone also are the days when the baby's father did the "honorable" thing and married the mother. The fact that the majority of Americans found Dan Quayle's criticism of unwed mothers offensive attests to the magnitude of the change in traditional values that has occurred.

Today, even though women still receive lower wages than men and, unlike their husbands, are usually adversely affected financially by divorce, they no longer feel compelled to marry or stay married for purely economic reasons. Nor, apparently, do the majority of divorced men feel compelled to support the children they have fathered. Two thirds of divorced women receive no child support from their husbands, and never-married mothers fare even worse—80 percent receive no financial support at all. For those who do receive support, the payments are often too low or too sporadic to improve the family's economic situation.

Economic Factors. William J. Wilson, professor of sociology and public policy at the University of Chicago, contends that high rates of illegitimacy and single-parent families, especially in poor black communities, have little to do with the availability or level of welfare benefits. He argues that male joblessness "could be the single most important factor underlying the rise in unwed mothers among poor black women."[6] High mortality and prison incarceration rates have combined with high unemployment rates to produce a shrinking pool of "marriageable" black men—men who can support a family.

Studies show a strong connection between favorable economic conditions and marriage for all Americans. In the inner city, researchers report, "young men . . . with steady work are two times as likely to marry the mother of their first child."[7] According to these experts, a better economic environment will have a profound effect on the moral climate of the community.

To a great extent, the current high rate of unwed-parent and single-parent black families reflects the hopelessness that many poor young black people feel about their future. Unlike middle-class young people, whose college or work plans would be disrupted by an unplanned pregnancy, many poor young people are so pessimistic about their future that they see little reason to delay childbearing. Some economists believe that "the most important intervention one could make today would be to change the employment situation of young men."[8]

Family Values and Government Policy. If, as most experts believe, family composition is a key determinant of poverty and welfare dependency, then what can or should the government do to reverse this? Journalist Ellis Cose advises:

"The political system, we must remember, is intended not to change the nation's morality, but to reflect it. And though the society is far from agreement on what to do about marriage, everyone agrees that children de-

serve a chance. If parents are increasingly unable to give them one, we must find more ways for government to help."[9]

The Children's Defense Fund suggests increasing government spending for early childhood education programs like Head Start, expanding the Job Corps program for disadvantaged youth, increasing AFDC benefits to reflect the current high cost of living, increasing support to all working poor families, and establishing a national child support system to force negligent fathers to assume financial responsibility for their children. According to the Children's Defense Fund, these policies would help strengthen families by keeping them out of poverty.[10]

Charles Murray, a fellow at the American Enterprise Institute, a conservative research institute, believes, however, that the demise of stable families among young poor people is a "social tragedy" that demands a radical change in government policy. He states: "My proposition is that illegitimacy is the single most important social problem of our time—more important than crime, drugs, poverty, illiteracy, welfare, or homelessness because it drives everything else." He warns that neither more social programs nor work programs will entirely reverse this behavior. He suggests that government policies should reflect the principle that "to bring a baby into the world when one is not emotionally or financially equipped to be a parent is profoundly irresponsible, and the government will no longer subsidize it."[11] Murray's prescription is severe: Cut off all benefits to single mothers, with the exception of medical insurance for their children. He argues that this policy would encourage independence, responsibility, and hard work, values that he believes most Americans uphold.

A teenage father visits his little girl after school on Long Island, New York. Not ready to take on the responsibility of a family, he does not live with her.

Current Welfare Policies. Although the total elimination of AFDC does not have wide support, policies that restrict benefits to unwed and single parents are becoming more common. In New Jersey and Georgia, welfare mothers no longer receive the $64-a-month increase previously allowed if an additional child is born while they are on aid. Many states now require teenage mothers to live with a parent or guardian while collecting benefits.

Conservative analyst Douglas J. Besharov is not confident that these policies will work. He thinks that rewarding positive behavior, rather than further depriving poor families of aid, may reap more results. He states: "Tangible rewards for doing the right thing can uplift and encourage; penalties threaten to discourage recipients who may already feel psychologically beaten down."[12] Proposals to reward recipients if they marry— called "wedfare" or "bridefare"—are currently being examined in several states.

Some legislators have suggested that welfare benefits be linked to the recipients' use of birth control. In Maryland, Governor Donald Schaefer proposed that welfare recipients be required to use Norplant, a birth control implant system that is effective for as long as five years, as a condition for receiving benefits. In Tennessee, legislators wanted to pay welfare recipients a bonus of $500 for getting Norplant and $50 for each year they stayed on the birth control system.

Although not all of these proposals have become laws yet, they indicate a growing acceptance of the government's authority to regulate the fertility of poor women. Supporters argue that if the government is required to support the children of poor single women, it also has the right to decide how many of these children will be born. Critics, however, warn that allowing the government to decide who can have children is dangerous to the individual liberty of American citizens.

It is still too early to tell whether welfare policies aimed at encouraging marriage will have any effect on the number of single-parent families or their dependence on welfare. Some experts believe that the radical transformation the American family has undergone in the past few decades will not be reversed by bonuses or penalties. Improving the economic prospects for both men and women, however, will help more families avoid or escape poverty. Whether they marry or not, an employed mother and father will have a better chance of supporting their children. Economist Mary Jo Bane advises that "the problem of poverty should be addressed by devoting attention to employment rather than hand-wringing about the decline of the family." [13]

In keeping with the current emphasis on demanding more personal responsibility in family planning in return for benefits, state and federal governments are also requiring that AFDC recipients make every possible effort to achieve financial independence through employment. The goal of transforming AFDC from a permanent cash assistance program to a temporary transition-to-work program has broad support among legislators, taxpayers, and recipients. President Bill Clinton hoped that increased work requirements, job training programs, and services to working welfare recipients would break the cycle of long-term dependency.

Dependency, Work, and Welfare

During the 1992 presidential campaign, President Clinton told voters that "welfare should be a second chance, not a way of life. . . . I want to erase the stigma of welfare for good by restoring a simple, dignified principle: No one who can work can stay on welfare forever."[1]

Welfare Dependency. For many poor single women and their children, AFDC is a temporary measure that relieves the economic hardship brought on by divorce, separation, or loss of income. The mother who is able to leave welfare after only a few years has usually entered the system as a result of divorce. She has often completed high school, has some work history, and is the parent of older children. Welfare helps her get back on her feet until remarriage, employment, adequate child support, or a combination of all three make it possible for her to become self-sufficient.

President Bill Clinton speaks on health and welfare issues at the National Governors' Association in February, 1993. He advocates getting people off welfare and into productive jobs.

A growing percentage of recipients, however, remain mired in poverty and trapped in welfare dependency for many years. These recipients usually began having children and receiving welfare when they were in their teens, have not graduated from high school, have little or no work experience, and have never been married.

Some analysts insist that only a small number of AFDC recipients remain on assistance for more than three years, while others argue that chronic welfare use is, indeed, a serious problem. Researchers can reach different conclusions about welfare dependency because welfare use is not always continuous. Many people receive aid for several years, go off assistance, and then return to the rolls for another stay. Taking into account this kind of cyclical dependence, a recent study concluded that while about 40 percent of recipients leave and stay off welfare after a few years, the remainder are dependent on aid for an average of about eight years.[2]

Some analysts argue that welfare dependency has grown because the system does not demand enough personal initiative and responsibility from recipients. They say that lax work requirements permit too many recipients to collect welfare indefinitely. According to this point of view, welfare both entices single mothers not to work and, by extending cash and medical benefits to nonworking single parents, devalues the effort and labor of those who work without government support.

Many welfare experts disagree with the view that AFDC benefits encourage single mothers not to work. A myriad of obstacles, they say, stand in the way of self-sufficiency. These include educational deficiencies, racial discrimination, lack or high cost of available child care, and minimal job opportunities. The most significant barrier to the self-support of single parents is the scarcity of jobs that pay enough to support a family. Many people believe that dependence on welfare is the result of our current low-wage economy. "Dependency," says Senator Daniel Patrick Moynihan, "is becoming the sort of characteristic problem of the post-industrial age, just as unemployment was the absolutely baffling and very destabilizing problem of the industrial age."[3]

New Expectations. According to a 1992 survey, very few Americans wish to eliminate welfare altogether. A majority, however, do favor replacing welfare with government-funded jobs.[4] While not without compassion for those less fortunate, most Americans believe that those who are capable should contribute to their own or their family's support. Single adults who are not disabled or do not have children, for example, are generally expected to support themselves. Similar expectations for single women with children are shifting the course of welfare policy away from dependency and toward employment.

AFDC was first created to allow poor single mothers to stay home and care for their children—an activity that was considered of value for all of society. Women were not expected to work and, until the mid-1960s, only a minority of women worked outside the home. Today, by contrast, more than half of all married mothers work and almost half of all single mothers are self-supporting. Since there is growing evidence that children of working mothers are as well adjusted as those whose mothers do not work, many legislators and policy experts contend that single women with children can no longer be excused from the expectations our society has for other working-age adults. As one critic said, "Why should the [welfare] mother be exempted by the system from the pressures that must affect everyone else's decision to work?"[5]

Welfare and Work. There are many reasons why AFDC recipients do not work or are not looking for work.

Some, like many other parents, want to stay home to care for their young children; some simply don't want to work; some are overwhelmed by the depression, passivity, and hopelessness that frequently accompany life on welfare; some are not qualified for work; some cannot find child care; some cannot find work. Many find that a job doesn't improve their financial status.

The choice between full-time welfare and full-time employment is not always an easy one for single mothers to make. The mother who is undereducated, unskilled, and unmarried is going to have a hard time finding a job that will adequately support her family. Because her skill level is low, she has limited employment options and will probably have to settle, at least at first, for a job that may not pay as much as her welfare grant does. Because she typically receives no support from her child's father, she will have to depend on this low salary to pay all her household expenses.

She will also have to pay for work-related expenses, including child care if she has young children, transportation to and from work, work clothes, and so on. She will have additional emotional and physical pressures as she tries to balance work and parenting responsibilities. Because many jobs currently do not provide employees with medical insurance, she must hope that neither she nor her children get sick.

Welfare, on the other hand, not only allows this single mother to be a full-time parent, but it also assures her family of important benefits that she may well lose if she works full-time, including medical insurance, housing subsidies, and food stamps. For many single mothers, choosing between work and welfare is difficult, since it is very likely that, in either case, she is going to be poor.

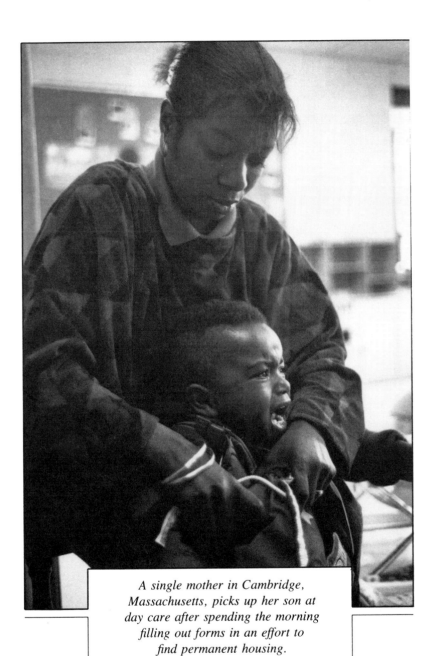

A single mother in Cambridge, Massachusetts, picks up her son at day care after spending the morning filling out forms in an effort to find permanent housing.

One option she has is to do both—collect welfare and work. Some welfare recipients do this by working "under the table" or by accepting money from relatives or friends to help pay for household expenses and not reporting this income to their welfare departments. Sociologists Christopher Jenks and Kathryn Edin, wondering how welfare mothers survive on such low monthly grants, studied fifty AFDC families in Cook County, Illinois. In this study, none of the recipients claimed that welfare was her sole income. Most of their outside income came from absent fathers, boyfriends, parents, siblings, and student loans, or from unreported work of various kinds—baby-sitting, catering, sewing, and bartending. A few worked regular jobs under different names, and a few were involved in illegal activities.[6]

Although some people consider this kind of behavior a form of welfare fraud, most welfare mothers consider it survival. As one welfare mother explains: "Many of us take money under the table for odd jobs,and cash from generous friends to help support our families. We don't report this money to the Aid to Families with Dependent Children because we can't afford to. Any cash we get, even birthday money from grandparents, is deducted from the already minuscule benefits. We're allowed between $1,000 and $3,000 in assets including savings and property, automobiles and home furnishings. We are told that if we have more than that amount, we should be able to sell some things and live for a year from the proceeds. Can you imagine living on $3,000 for a year?"[7]

AFDC recipients can work and also legally collect welfare for a period of time. While still requiring that working recipients meet their income eligibility requirements, states must also disregard a certain amount of earned monthly income before benefits are reduced or terminated. The first $90 of income a month is regarded as a work expense and is not counted. In addition, the "30 and ⅓ rule" stipulates that $30 of income a month for twelve months is disregarded and one third of additional earnings for the first four consecutive months of employment is also disregarded. Recipients are also allowed to deduct some monthly child care expenses. These benefits are designed to allow recipients to enter the workforce and gain valuable work experience and skills without completely eliminating their benefits.

The Family Support Act. For many years, the government has required that certain AFDC recipients, usually those with older children, work toward the goal of employment. In 1967, states were required to implement the Work Incentive program (WIN). WIN allowed recipients to work without losing all of their benefits, and required recipients with children over the age of six to register for employment opportunities. In 1981, states were permitted to devise their own work programs for recipients and, since that time, states have created many "workfare" programs, some voluntary and some mandatory, in an effort to move AFDC clients off the welfare rolls and into the workplace.

By the mid-1980s, widespread dissatisfaction with the existing workforce programs and growing concerns about long-term welfare dependency prompted Democratic and Republican legislators to work together to reform our welfare system. After numerous hearings, studies, and compromises, Congress passed the Family Support Act of 1988. This legislation emphasizes education, employment, child support enforcement, and family benefits so that more welfare families can become self-supporting.

The Jobs Opportunity and Basic Skills (JOBS) program, the centerpiece of the Family Support Act of 1988 and the latest welfare-to-work endeavor, aims to help recipients who leave AFDC make the transition from welfare to work more easily. JOBS helps recipients overcome common barriers to self-sufficiency by providing extensive educational and training services, child care allowances, and extended medical and child care benefits after leaving. Senator Moynihan, architect of the Family Support Act, hopes that the act will transform welfare from a permanent state of poverty to a "transition to employment."[8]

The U.S. Department of Health and Human Services believes that its JOBS program will help break the cycle of welfare poverty that affects so many Americans. "Through job training, work, and education, welfare recipients gain the opportunity to break the cycle of dependency and move into the working world. The potential benefits of achieving self-sufficiency through employment include increased income, economic options, enhanced self-worth, and serving as needed role models for children, as well as contributing to society through work and payment of taxes."[9]

Jobs Opportunity and Basic Skills Program (JOBS). The Family Support Act of 1988 requires states to operate JOBS programs and provides matching federal money to help fund such programs. By 1995, 20 percent of eligible recipients must participate in one of four basic programs: education, which includes high school equivalency test preparation, literacy improvement, or English proficiency; on-the-job training; public or private employment; or community service.

Although most mothers with children under the age of three are exempt from participating, states do have the option of requiring mothers whose youngest child is one year old to enroll in its program. A recipient must be assigned a counselor to devise a program that meets

At a government-sponsored training center in Little Rock, Arkansas, teenagers learn a trade that could help them escape a life of poverty.

her needs and is appropriate for her skill level. Participants are required to spend up to twenty hours a week in the selected program, and if child care is needed, the state must guarantee payments, through vouchers, reimbursement, or contracts, up to a maximum of $175 per month per child or $200 if the child is under the age of two. If a recipient earns too much money at a job to continue to qualify for AFDC, the state must continue her child care allowances and Medicaid benefits for one year.

Implementation. The federal government earmarked $1.3 billion for JOBS programs in 1995. A sluggish economy and tight state budgets, however, have delayed full implementation of the program. President Clinton's welfare reform task force recommended that the federal government increase funding to the states so they can provide more training and educational services to recipients.

In addition to inadequate revenues to fund their JOBS programs, many states are finding it difficult to find jobs for their clients. A. Sidney Johnson III, executive director of the American Public Welfare Association, claims that "job opportunities for those who graduate from our training programs simply do not exist today."[10]

Workfare Does Not Work. There are many critics of current workfare programs. Some people believe that the government is punishing single mothers by forcing them to take low-wage jobs. Former welfare recipient and author Theresa Funicello, for instance, is adamantly opposed to any policy that requires welfare mothers to work. She claims that "the job and training programs so prevalent today are rarely much more than mechanisms of torture."[11] Single women with children, she states, already work full-time as parents. This author also decries the fact that while welfare mothers are being forced to work, widowed mothers receive survivor's benefits for themselves and their children without being criticized for dependent behavior.

Other critics charge that there simply are not enough decent jobs to raise the standard of living for single mothers and their children. How, they wonder, can welfare mothers find full-time employment at a wage that ensures economic security when national unemployment rates are about 7 percent, corporations are downsizing, manufacturing jobs are declining, and the numbers of the working poor are growing?[12] Christopher Jenks and Kathryn Edin agree: "Single mothers do not turn to welfare because they are pathologically dependent on handouts or unusually reluctant to work—they do so because they cannot get jobs that pay better than welfare."[13]

Workfare Can Succeed. Although there is a general sense that welfare-to-work programs are not very successful in reducing the welfare rolls or long-term dependency, the results of one recent study are cautiously positive. The Manpower Demonstration Research Corporation, established by the Ford Foundation and six federal agencies in 1974 to study welfare policy, recently reported that many programs do increase participants' earnings and, despite the costs of job training and other services, ultimately do save the government money. The study found that job search services that quickly match up a recipient with an available job, and educational and skills programs that improve job readiness, help many recipients leave welfare. The study did warn that underfunded programs are the least effective, and that even the most successful programs do not move large numbers of recipients off welfare and into the workplace.[14]

Despite the difficulty mothers experience in balancing work and family responsibilities, as well as the fact that most of the jobs participants initially get do not increase their annual income much beyond their previous AFDC grants, many participants report surprisingly positive changes in their lives. One welfare mother, who spent three years on welfare before finding a job, claims that her outlook on life has improved: "I'm just as broke now because I've got more things to pay . . . But I'm happy. It's my money. I've earned it."[15]

This, claims journalist Mickey Kaus, author of *The End of Equality,* is because work—even a low-wage job—has intrinsic value for families and communities. Working adults are participants in, and contributors to, the larger society. The children of working parents, in turn, learn the value of responsibility, obligation, and hard work. Unlike welfare, work is active, not passive. Work gains respect, not scorn; work implies organization, not disorder. This critic of our welfare system believes that AFDC should be replaced with a system of government-funded work programs.[16]

While some critics of welfare suggest making welfare even less attractive than it is now, numerous experts believe that the solution is to make work more attractive by ensuring that employed Americans, particularly those who are supporting families, are not poor. Policies that would "make work pay" include increasing and expanding the Earned Income Tax Credit for low-income families with children, raising the minimum wage, and providing universal medical coverage.

The Future of Welfare. Even when states fully implement the Family Support Act's JOBS programs in 1995, only 20 percent of eligible recipients will be required to participate. If the goal is to move large numbers of welfare recipients off the rolls, the JOBS program alone is not the answer. In fact, the Congressional Budget Office projects that only about 50,000 recipients over the course of five years will leave welfare as a result of JOBS.[17] How, then, can more substantial reductions in the number of people dependent on welfare be achieved?

Many legislators favor limiting the amount of time that an individual can remain on aid. Vermont, Florida, and Wisconsin have sought permission from the federal government to impose such time limits in their states. Vermont, for example, has proposed a thirty-month benefit limit—with the guarantee of a government-funded job if recipients have not found a job by the time their eligibility has ended. California has a harsher solution: a 25 percent reduction in AFDC benefits to those who are still on welfare after six months.

President Clinton, who promised to "end welfare as we know it," appointed a task force to study and formulate a plan to reform our current welfare system. Many of the proposals would no doubt reinforce the Family Support Act's goal of increasing self-sufficiency through work and training, demanding child support from absent fathers, and extending noncash benefits to welfare mothers after they leave assistance. Time limits, government jobs, the elimination of all cash assistance, and a national child support program were but a few of the numerous ideas aimed at reducing welfare dependency and single-parent poverty currently discussed at both the state and federal levels of government.

Reforming the Welfare System

During the summer of 1993, President Clinton's task force, composed of about thirty policy experts from nine federal agencies, began hearing recommendations for welfare reform from legislators, welfare specialists, and child advocates. Some of the most personal and compelling testimony the task force heard came from AFDC recipients themselves. Describing the system as insensitive and impersonal, one mother of three children told the panel that she is often treated as if "I don't have feelings, children, commitments, ideas or choices. . . . I am insulted and rushed through. . . . Someone needs to pay attention to me. Who am I? What are my skills? Am I educated? What are my goals? Help us move forward instead of holding us back."[1]

What About the Fathers? A common complaint from expert and AFDC witnesses alike was that, while welfare mothers are the object of state cutbacks, work requirements, and public criticism, absent fathers are shirking their parental and financial responsibilities and are getting away with it. Although required by law to pay child support to the state if their children receive AFDC benefits, very few of these fathers do. In Wisconsin, for example, the state with one of the highest child support collection rates in the country, only about 13 percent of "welfare" fathers pay child support. Estimating that the government is losing about $20 to $30 billion a year in support payments due single mothers, and citing the difficulty state agencies have experienced in locating missing fathers who move from state to state or job to job, several witnesses recommended that a national system of child support enforcement be established and that the Internal Revenue Service be put in charge of child support collections.

Enforcing Child Support Obligations. In order for agencies or families to collect child support, there must be a support order that stipulates the amount of money the absent parent must contribute each week. This order usually originates from legal divorce or separation proceedings. Although the process is more complicated, support orders are also issued to fathers who are not married to the mother of their child.

Local child support enforcement agencies in each state help collect payments from delinquent fathers by locating missing fathers, obtaining support awards from the courts, and, if the father's name is not on the child's birth certificate, helping mothers through the process of establishing paternity so they may then obtain a court order for child support.

Federal laws allow states to take child support payments from a delinquent father's paycheck, known as wage garnishment, as well as from his state and federal tax refunds. In an effort to increase collections, states are also employing a variety of tactics to recover support payments from delinquent fathers, including advertising "deadbeat dads" in newspapers and on television, contracting with private collection agencies, and publicly arresting delinquent fathers. In Wisconsin, fathers who do not meet their obligations are given three-choices: pay up, perform public service, or go to jail. As a result of this intensive effort, collections have increased by 237 percent.[2]

Signing over child support payments and alimony to the state government is a stipulation of welfare eligibility. If these payments exceed the monthly welfare grant, then the mother is no longer eligible for welfare and the payments are sent directly to the family. In 1992, however, only about 7 percent of AFDC recipients left welfare because they began receiving regular and adequate child support payments.[3] Although there are fathers who could pay more than they do but refuse to for one reason or another, a significant number of fathers whose children are supported by welfare are unemployed or have very low incomes themselves. Some policy experts advocate the establishment of a national insurance system to help support children of all single parents.

Child Support Assurance. Numerous public welfare specialists believe that the government should protect children whose fathers are absent in much the same way it protects children whose fathers are deceased or unemployed. The creation of a child support assurance program, a proposal made some years ago by David T. Ellwood, co-chair of the president's task force, could ultimately transform AFDC from public assistance to a form of social insurance for children. In theory, a child-support assurance program would provide a guaranteed annual income to the children of all single parents, regardless of the mother's employment or financial status.

A homeless father in Austin, Texas, stands at the side of a street asking for work and assistance.

Some propose that a standard of $2,500 for one child and $1,000 for additional children be fixed. To fund the program, the federal government, ostensibly through the Internal Revenue Service, would be in charge of collecting child support payments. For families in which the absent parent was missing, delinquent, or unable to pay the full amount of the annual benefit level, the federal government would make up the difference. In either case, the children of single parents would be guaranteed a minimum level of support.

Supporters believe that, by providing a reliable source of child support, this plan would reduce the high rate of poverty that single-parent families experience; prevent many single parents from having to go on welfare; and provide more work incentives than our current welfare system does because single parents would receive the same level of support regardless of their earned income. By combining child support assurance and part-time or full-time earnings, a single parent could more easily escape poverty and welfare dependency. In addition, child support assurance would not be considered welfare, but an entitlement for all children in single-parent families. This, Ellwood claims, would end the isolation, stigma, and sense of failure that many AFDC recipients now experience.[4]

Time Limits for AFDC Eligibility. In response to the growth of chronic poverty and welfare dependency, especially in urban areas, many policy analysts are recommending that the government limit the time that a recipient can receive AFDC benefits. President Clinton urged a limit of two years, during which time recipients would be trained, educated, and made "work ready" by enhancing the current JOBS program. Others within his administration supported this idea and hoped to transform welfare from a permanent life in poverty to a transition to employment.

Any reform proposal that limits the time a person can collect welfare will have to address several issues and take into account a variety of situations: If the mother has another child within the two-year period, does she automatically qualify for another two years? Should a mother of a two-year-old child be forced to work full-time? What if she does not have adequate child care available or her child becomes sick? Will the government simply abandon the children of those who, at the end of their time on welfare, have failed, refused, or not been able to find a job?

Government-Funded Jobs. One idea outlined by Senator David Boren of Oklahoma and other lawmakers has been to put millions of unemployed Americans, including welfare recipients, to work by creating a public jobs program similar to that overseen by the Works Progress Administration (WPA) during the Great Depression. Believing that public assistance acted like a "narcotic" on the needy, President Roosevelt substituted government-paid jobs for public assistance. The WPA put more than 8 million unemployed American men and women to work, including laborers, high school students, writers, and actors.

Journalist Mickey Kaus would like to see welfare eliminated altogether and replaced by guaranteed government jobs. He envisions a system in which "single mothers (and anyone else) who needed money would not be given a check. They would be given free day care for their children. And they would be given the location of a government job site. If they showed up and worked, they'd be paid for their work."[5] Those who refused work would receive no other help, aside from private charities, soup kitchens, and shelters. Kaus believes his idea would eventually reduce chronic poverty and welfare dependency by promoting civic pride and social responsibility. "Even children of single mothers," he says, "would grow up in homes structured by the rhythms and discipline of work."[6] Fewer young women, he predicts, would view single parenthood as a viable option if their only source of support came from full-time work instead of a monthly check.

Although Kaus's prescription for reducing welfare dependency and single-parent families is probably too harsh to be implemented by our government, many people are in favor of a guaranteed job program for needy Americans. Some, including President Clinton, recommend combining time-limited welfare benefits with a guarantee of a government job for those unable to find work after their benefits have been terminated.

Investing in the Youth of America. Child poverty, infant mortality, and teen pregnancy rates in the United States are at their highest levels in decades. Citing evidence that chronic poverty often robs children of their potential to become successful students, parents, and workers, many people believe that our government should increase spending for both preschool education and job training programs, and should establish a national minimum welfare benefit level to reduce the dismal poverty so many AFDC families experience.

Research demonstrates that extending services to the poor at early stages of need can prevent long-term and more expensive forms of dependence. The Manpower Research Development Corporation reports that every $1 spent on immunizations against childhood diseases saves $10 in future medical costs, every $1 spent on prenatal care for low-income women saves $3.38 in health care in a child's first year; every $1 spent on Job

Corps training for disadvantaged youth saves $1.45 in crime, drug abuse, and welfare costs; every $1 spent on preschool education saves $4.75 in special education, public assistance, and crime; and every $1 spent on employment training for welfare mothers saves $3 in AFDC costs.[7]

Programs that aim to reduce the number of teenage pregnancies and births, particularly to those who are not married, would also provide huge savings to taxpayers. The government currently spends about $25 billion to support families begun by single teen parents, who are rarely financially or emotionally equipped to support a family.[8] In 1993, the country's overall teen pregnancy and birthrates rose for the fifth year in a row. Schools, churches, and social agencies around the country are responding to this crisis by offering a variety of programs to young people. Many school and community-based programs focus on helping teens resist peer pressure, delay sexual activity, improve self-esteem, and develop career and life goals. In some schools and clinics, teens who are sexually active can receive birth control information as well as contraceptives to prevent pregnancy and sexually transmitted diseases.

Many experts, however, are distressed that even intensive programs are failing to reduce the rate of teen pregnancy, especially among poor young people. This, claim some social workers, is because the effects of poverty, despair, and diminished economic prospects far outweigh those of positive social programs. "What we know without a doubt is the more a person has to look forward to in life," says one analyst, "the more careful he is about his sexual behavior."[9]

Visions for the Future. Social welfare programs extend a helping hand to all Americans so that we can participate in the economic and social life of our society. So-

Boys stand in the hallway that leads to the apartments where they are growing up in Harlem, New York City.

cial insurance programs allow citizens to maintain economic stability when they are unable to work because of age, disability, or job loss; antipoverty programs aim to equalize job and educational opportunity for disadvantaged citizens; medical insurance for the elderly and the poor provide basic medical care for those without insurance through employment; and welfare programs, including AFDC, food stamps, nutrition programs, and housing subsidies, help low-income people meet their basic needs. The federal government also helps its citizens by granting tax deductions for home mortgages, low-interest loans to businesses, and funds for public education, libraries, public parks, and highways.

"Social-welfare policies are about human beings," says author and social activist Leslie Dunbar. "They are about the national interest, also, if anyone can distinguish between the two. But first of all, about people's lives. They are about children, and their chances to grow and find some joy and fulfillment in life; and about grown-ups, and their opportunities to get a fair share and, as a result, participate in the public life of this democracy." [10]

While serious disagreements remain about the effectiveness and desirability of our current system, most Americans believe that the government has a fundamental responsibility to help disadvantaged children and adults lead productive lives. There are many ways in which the government can help poor people: increase welfare benefits so that children are not living in abject poverty, create more jobs so that those who are able to work can earn a living, provide universal health care so that every American can afford medical care, provide tax credits to poor working families, and invest more money in education and job training so that all citizens will be equipped to become self-supporting.

Americans also expect citizens to make every effort possible to help themselves, and we want our social policies to reflect the basic values that our society holds: family responsibility, individual initiative, and hard work and effort. As a result, many people believe that individuals, rather than the government, are primarily responsible for their own and their family's support. We expect our fellow citizens to adopt behaviors that will improve their chances for economic stability, such as delaying childbirth, completing an education, and working hard and regularly at a job to provide for their families. Single women with children are no longer exempt from work expectations, nor are absent fathers exempt from contributing to the support of their children.

Although preventing families from needing assistance and helping greater numbers of families leave our welfare system is a goal that, so far, has eluded Democratic and Republican administrations alike, President Clinton is determined to overhaul the system so that fewer families will spend their lives in poverty and isolation. States throughout the country have already enacted significant reforms to their programs. While it is too early to tell what specific changes will be implemented nationally, the most likely ingredients of the Clinton administration's welfare reform package will include time limitations, guaranteed government-funded jobs, more rigorous child support enforcement policies, greater economic incentives, and extensive health care provisions.

Whatever reforms are made to our welfare system, one thing is certain: They will need to be reexamined on a regular basis. Welfare and society are inextricably linked, and the social and economic character of our nation will always be subject to change.

Notes

Chapter One

1. Sylvester Monroe, Tom Curry, and Sophronia Scott Gregory, "The Fire This Time," *Time,* May 11, 1992, p 22.
2. Andrew Hacker, *Two Nations Black and White, Separate, Hostile and Unequal* (New York: Charles Scribner's Sons, 1992), p. 84.
3. Thomas Sancton, "How to Get America Off the Dole," *Time,* May 25, 1992, p. 44.
4. Sancton, p. 45.
5. Sancton, p. 44.
6. Lance Morrow, "But Seriously, Folks," *Time,* June 1, 1992, p. 30.
7. William J. Bennett, "The Moral Origins of the Urban Crisis," *The Wall Street Journal,* May 3, 1992, p. 8.
8 David Whitman, "The War on Welfare Dependency," *U.S. News and World Report,* April 20, 1992, p. 35.
9. "A Mother's Message," An Interview with Marion Wright Edelman, *Newsweek,* June 8, 1992, p. 27.
10. Michael B. Katz, *The Undeserving Poor: From the War on Poverty to the War on Welfare* (New York: Pantheon Books, 1989), p. 165.

Chapter Two

1. Walter I. Trattner, *From Poor Law to Welfare State: A History of Social Welfare in America* (New York: Free Press, 1974), p. 21.
2. Ruth Sidel, *Women and Children Last: The Plight of Poor Women in Affluent America* (New York: Penguin Books, 1992), p. 80.
3. Lela B. Costin and Charles A. Rapp, *Child Welfare: Policies and Practice* (New York: McGraw-Hill, 1984), p. 162.
4. Trattner, p. 252.
5. Frances Fox Piven and Richard A. Cloward, *Regulating the Poor: The Functions of Public Welfare* (New York: Vintage Books, 1971), p. 76.
6. Piven and Cloward, p. 94.
7. Paul A. Levy, "The Durability of Supreme Court and Welfare Reforms of the 1960s," *Social Service Review*, Vol. 66, No. 2, The University of Chicago Press, June 1992, p. 227.
8. Levy, p. 231.
9. Trattner, p. 285.
10. Lyndon B. Johnson, remarks at a Democratic party fundraising dinner, Detroit, June 26, 1964, reprinted in Marrin E. Gettleman and David Mermelstein, *The Great Society Reader* (New York: Random House, 1967), p. 21.

Chapter Three

1. David E. Rosenbaum, "Answer: Cut Entitlements. Question: But How?" *The New York Times*, June 8, 1993.
2. Theodore R. Marmor, Jerry L. Mashaw, and Philip L. Harvey, *America's Misunderstood Welfare: Persistent Myths, Enduring Realities* (New York: Basic Books, 1990), p. 34.
3. David Whitman, "War on Welfare Dependency," *U.S. News and World Report*, April 20, 1992, p. 35.

Chapter Four

1. John E. Schwarz and Thomas J. Volgy, *Forgotten Americans: Forty Million Working Poor in America* (New York: W.W. Norton & Co., 1992), p. 39.

2. John E. Schwarz and Thomas J. Volgy, "Above the Poverty Line—But Poor," *The Nation*, February 15, 1993, p. 191.
3. Harrel R. Rodgers, Jr., *Poverty Amid Plenty: A Political and Economic Analysis* (New York: Random House, 1974), p. 30.
4. Guy Gugliotta, "Drawing the Poverty Line: A Calculation of Necessity and Self-Image," *The Washington Post*, May 10, 1993 (located in *Newsbank* [Microform], Welfare, 1993, 15:E3, fiche).
5. Ibid.
6. *The Economic Report to the President: 1964.* (Washington DC: Government Printing Office, 1965), p. 7.
7. The Children's Defense Fund, *The State of America's Children, 1992* (The Children's Defense Fund: Washington, DC, 1993), p. 26.
8. Suzanne Coil, *The Poor in America* (Englewood Cliffs, NJ: Julian Messner, 1989), p. 52.
9. William Julius Wilson, *The Truly Disadvantaged: The Inner City, the Underclass and Public Policy* (Chicago: University of Chicago Press, 1987), p. 8.
10. Lawrence Mead, *The New Politics of Poverty* (New York: Basic Books, 1992), p. 11.
11. Dale Maharidge, "The Rural Poor Get Poorer," *The Nation*, January 13, 1992, p. 10.
12. John E. Schwarz and Thomas J. Volgy, "Above the Poverty Line—But Poor," *The Nation*, February 15, 1993, p. 192.

Chapter Five

1. Lance Morrow, "But Seriously, Folks," *Time*, June 1, 1992, p. 30.
2. Barbara Dafoe Whitehead, "Dan Quayle Was Right," *Atlantic Monthly*, April 1993, p. 62.
3. David T. Ellwood, *Poor Support: Poverty in the American Family.* (New York: Basic Books, 1988), p. 22.
4. Mickey Kaus, *The End of Equality,* (New York: Basic Books, 1993), p. 117.
5. Ellwood, p. 57.
6. William Julius Wilson, *The Truly Disadvantaged: The Inner City, the Underclass, and Public Policy* (Chicago: University of Chicago Press, 1987), p. 73.

7. Don L. Boroughs, "Love and Money," *U.S. News and World Report,* October 19, 1992, p. 56.
8. Boroughs, p. 58.
9. Ellis Cose, "Protecting the Children," *Newsweek,* August 30, 1993, p. 29.
10. The Children's Defense Fund, *The State of America's Children 1992* (Washington, DC: The Children's Defense Fund, 1993).
11. Charles Murray, "The Coming White Underclass," *The Wall Street Journal,* October 29, 1993, p. A14.
12. Douglas J. Besharov, "Beware of Unintended Consequences," *Public Welfare,* Spring 1992, p. 19.
13. Mary Jo Bane, "Household Composition and Poverty," in *Fighting Poverty: What Works and What Doesn't,* eds. Sheldon H. Danziger and Daniel H. Weinberg (Cambridge, MA: Harvard University Press, 1986), p. 231.

Chapter Six

1. Remarks of Arkansas Governor Bill Clinton at Georgetown University, October 23, 1991.
2. Jeffrey L. Katz, "Sampling Welfare Users," *CQ Researcher,* January 22, 1994, p. 122.
3. Thomas Sancton, "How to Get America Off the Dole," *Time,* May 25, 1992, p. 47.
4. Sancton, p. 45.
5. Charles Murray, *Losing Ground: American Social Policy: 1960–1980* (New York: Basic Books, 1984), p. 231.
6. Christopher Jenks, *Rethinking Social Policy: Race, Poverty, and the Underclass* (New York: HarperPerennial, 1992), pp. 204–208.
7. Theresa McCrary, "Getting Off the Welfare Carousel," *Newsweek,* December 6, 1993, p. 11.
8. Oona Sullivan, "Research Sheds New Light on Welfare Reforms," *Ford Foundation Letter,* Fall 1991, p. 11.
9. U.S. Department of Health and Human Services, Administration for Children and Families, "Factsheet: Job Opportunities and Basic Skills Training (JOBS) Program," March 1992.
10. Kenneth Jost, "Welfare Reform," *CQ Researcher,* April 10, 1992, p. 327.

11. Theresa Funicello, *The Tyranny of Kindness: Dismantling the Welfare System to End Poverty in America* (New York: Atlantic Monthly Press, 1993), p. 272.

12. Richard A. Cloward and Frances Fox Piven, "The Fraud of Workfare," *The Nation,* May 24, 1993, pp. 693–697.

13. Jenks, p. 204.

14. Judith M. Gueron and Edward Pauly, *From Work to Welfare* (New York: The Russell Sage Foundation, 1991).

15. Phoebe Wall Howard, "A Job, A Paycheck: A Dream Realized," *The Des Moines Register,* August 31, 1993 (located in *Newsbank* [Microform], Welfare, 1993, 27:D11, fiche).

16. Mickey Kaus, *The End of Equality* (New York: Basic Books, 1993).

17. Jeffrey L. Katz, "A Welcome But Unwieldy Idea? Putting an End to Welfare," *CQ Weekly Report,* February 27, 1993, p. 458.

Chapter Seven

1. Associated Press, "Mothers Tell U.S. Welfare Panel in Chicago of Their Hardships," *The Boston Globe,* August 12, 1993, p. 9.

2. Joe Klein, "Make the Daddies Pay," *Newsweek,* June 21, 1993, p. 33.

3. Dorien Friedman, "Why the Welfare Mess Gets Messier," *U.S. News and World Report,* November 25, 1991, p. 31.

4. David T. Ellwood, *Poor Support: Poverty in the American Family* (New York: Basic Books, 1988).

5. Mickey Kaus, "Yes, Something Will Work: Work," *Newsweek,* May 18, 1992, p. 38.

6. Ibid.

7. Susan B. Garland, "A Way Out of the Morass," *Businessweek: Reinventing America,* 1992, p. 104.

8. Ibid.

9. Sara Glazer, "Preventing Teen Pregnancy," *CQ Researcher,* May 14, 1993, p. 425.

10. Leslie Dunbar, *The Common Interest: How Our Social Welfare Policies Don't Work and What We Can Do About Them* (New York: Pantheon Books, 1988), p. x.

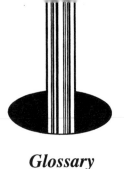

Glossary

absolute poverty: the lack of basic necessities, including food, shelter, and medical care, required for survival in a society.

Aid to Families with Dependent Children (AFDC): a cash assistance program for low-income single parents and children. AFDC-UP helps a limited number of poor two-parent families.

cash assistance program: any program that provides cash grants to beneficiaries. AFDC, SSI, and OASDI are examples of cash assistance programs.

entitlement program: broadly defined as any federal or state benefit program; more narrowly defined as a benefit program "earned" through financial contributions, such as Social Security, or special activities, such as Veterans' Benefits.

Family Support Act: the 1988 welfare reform package that requires states to enforce child support orders and offer job training, educational services, child care subsidies, and transitional medical insurance to AFDC recipients. The law also requires recipients, except those with very young children, to register and participate in educational and job-related activities.

Food Stamp Program: a national program available to low-income households that provides vouchers redeemable for food at most retail food stores.

general assistance: optional state cash assistance program for indigent individuals who do not qualify for any other government aid.

income support program: a cash assistance program for low-income individuals and families.

in-kind benefits: goods and services, including medical insurance, food stamps, housing assistance, and educational services associated with benefit programs.

means-tested programs: state and federal benefit programs that require verification of financial need for qualification.

Medicaid: state and federal program that provides medical insurance to low-income individuals and families.

Medicare: state and federal program that provides medical benefits to elderly citizens.

Old Age, Survivors, and Disability Insurance (OASDI): provides cash benefits to workers and their families when the worker becomes unable to work because of age, disability, or death. Popularly known as Social Security.

poverty line: the income figure, established yearly by the federal government and adjusted for family size, that denotes the minimum amount of money required to purchase life's basic necessities.

relative poverty: lack of income and resources available to most people in a society.

social insurance program: a cash assistance program that aims to protect working people from falling into poverty when they are no longer able to work because of age, disability, or unemployment. Survivor's benefits protect workers' families. Social Security, Workers' Compensation, and Unemployment Compensation are social insurance programs.

Supplementary Security Income (SSI): federal cash assistance program that assists low-income blind, disabled, and elderly people.

welfare: a term commonly used to describe programs aimed at alleviating conditions of poverty. AFDC, General Relief, and SSI are considered welfare programs.

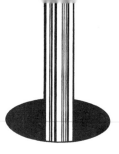

For Further
Information

Recommended Reading

Coil, Suzanne. *The Poor in America.* Englewood Cliffs, NJ: Julian Messner, 1989.

Edelman, Marian Wright. *Families in Peril.* Cambridge, MA: Harvard University Press, 1987.

Ellwood, David T. *Poor Support.* New York: Basic Books, 1988.

Jenks, Christopher. *Rethinking Social Policy: Race, Poverty and the Underclass.* New York: HarperPerennial, 1992.

Katz, Michael B. *The Undeserving Poor: From the War on Poverty to the War on Welfare.* New York: Pantheon Books, 1989.

Kaus, Mickey. *The End of Equality.* New York: Basic Books, 1992.

Mead, Lawrence M. *The New Politics of Poverty: The Nonworking Poor in America.* New York: Basic Books, 1992.

Schorr, Lisbeth, with Daniel Schorr. *Within Our Reach: Breaking the Cycle of Disadvantage.* New York: Anchor Press/ Doubleday, 1988.